Rooms for Improvement

Professional designs and decorating ideas made easy

Devised by Lloyd Atkinson
Written by Marina Henderson
Photography by Don Honeyman

SAMPSON LOW

Published by Sampson Low
Berkshire House, Queen Street, Maidenhead
Designed and produced for Sampson Low by
Intercontinental Book Productions
Copyright © 1975 Intercontinental Book Productions
Printed and bound in Italy

SBN 562 00017 8

CONTENTS

INTRODUCTION

What makes the décor of an ordinary room special? You don't need expensive furniture, a superb carpet or luxurious curtains to achieve that 'interior decorator' look. You need ideas—and this book is full of them. Here we show you some exciting new ways of dealing with the walls, doors, windows and floors of your house—the flat surfaces which make up the basic décor of any room but which often get overlooked in decorative schemes. They are the sort of ideas that you may have seen in glossy magazines and assumed that they could only be done by professional decorators. But anyone who has had some 'do-it-yourself' experience, or has done any home sewing, can carry out these projects.

Each of our thirty projects features a drawing or a photograph of the finished scheme, a list of materials and tools needed to carry it out, and simple step-by-step instructions, clearly and fully illustrated. Always read the description of the project right the way through the instructions before you start. You may often have to adapt the measurements and quantities we give to suit your rooms and it is important to make sure that you know and understand what is involved at every stage of the project. Check, too, that you have all the necessary equipment; not only the special equipment we list but everyday tools such as scissors that we have not always had room to include. For a professional finish, use the tips on basic decorating, pages 7-15.

Basic Tools

In any decorating job, there are certain tools that you should have. These are not only necessary to carry out the projects but will be useful for any work around the house. Don't economize too much—good tools properly looked after will outlast and out-perform cheap ones. Here are certain items of basic equipment for the painting, wallpapering, simple carpentry and sewing jobs we describe. In addition, you must have plenty of heavy-duty dustsheets, a good supply of cleaning cloths and a sturdy stepladder. Remember that it is possible to hire big items, such as extra stepladders or scaffolding boards, in most towns now, so check what you can hire before buying expensive equipment for which you'll find little use afterwards. We recommend an electric drill, but a hand drill does the job just as well—if with more effort!

Be conscientious about looking after your equipment. It is easy to ruin a paint brush by not cleaning it properly when you have completed a job. Follow the manufacturer's instructions when cleaning off different types of paint. Make sure that the blade of your saw is protected when stored, and is kept rust-free and sharp. Don't let anyone use your chisel as a screwdriver or handy paint-tin opener! The proper tools help you to achieve satisfactory results.

PAPERING and PAINTING EQUIPMENT. Below, from left to right, arranged on pasting table: cutting-in tool, 12, 25, 50 and 100mm paint brushes, paint-stripping knife, filling knife, sandpaper block, white spirit, pasting bucket, pasting brush, paperhanger's scissors, pencil, plumb line, roller and tray, masking tape, stripping knife, wire brush, paperhanging brush.

CARPENTRY and SEWING EQUIPMENT. Above, from left to right: tenon saw, padsaw, mitre box, spirit level, ratchet screwdriver, retractable rule, electric drill and bits (or hand drill), countersink, 450-570gm claw hammer, pin hammer, rigid rule, bevel-edge chisel, staple gun, sewing machine, dressmaking scissors, hop-up, pins, tape measure.

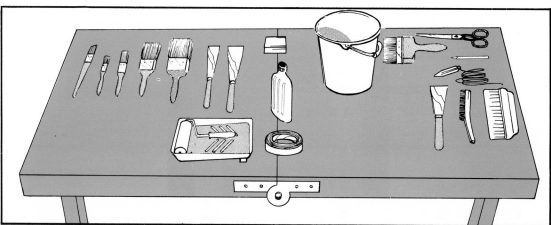

Design and Colour

Matching wallpaper and fabric help to give an illusion of greater space in this small bedroom. We show you how to make the roman blinds on page 28.

Take time to plan your overall décor. You may see a stunning new wallpaper that you fall in love with, but unless you are starting from scratch, you probably have carpets, curtains and loose covers that you can't afford to change in these expensive days. The new wallpaper may be what you have always wanted, but does it match the furnishings in your room?

Plan your room round its existing features, its function and its shape. To decorate a living-room where the family work and play in pale pastel shades and delicate fabrics is a waste of time and money. Fabric-hung walls are obviously not suitable for kitchens, where all the surfaces should be easily washable. If you have small children, be careful how you decorate the staircase wall: sticky hands can ruin anything!

Clever planning can help to disguise a room's awkward shape. A low-ceilinged room looks more spacious if you choose dark or patterned walls and a light-coloured ceiling. High ceilings will look lower if you decorate them in a dark shade and the walls in a lighter one. A square

box-like room becomes more interesting if you paint and paper it in the same colour or pattern throughout, ceiling included! See our project *Circus Top* (page 34) which was designed for just such a dining-room.

Small rooms can gain a new dimension if matching wallpaper and curtain fabrics are used and the woodwork painted in a toning shade. To square off a long, narrow room, decorate the end walls in a dark colour or pattern and the side walls in a lighter, toning shade. If you have a very dark room, do not be afraid of choosing a dark colour scheme. Paradoxically, this can make a room look lighter than a clear bright colour!

Colour is important. The best worked out plans can be ruined by using the wrong colours. We make colour suggestions in most of our projects but you may want to change these to suit your own taste. Remember that blues and greens are 'cold' colours and are best used in light, sunny rooms. If you want a warm effect, choose yellows, oranges, reds and browns.

The striking fabric has set the scheme for the whole room. The walls, painted in a plain, dark colour, act as a foil for the brightness and complexity of the design.

Whatever you decide, pick a basic colour and stick to it. You don't need to mix a lot of colours to give a colourful effect. One of the most attractive and practical ideas for a living-room is to decorate and furnish it in one colour throughout—but using a range of tones, from darkest to lightest. And one of the most luxurious ideas is an all-white room.

If you already have a vividly-patterned carpet or curtains, pick out the dominant colour in these and paint your walls to match it. Try not to mix patterns; it's seldom successful. Plain or matching fabrics look much better with a strongly patterned wallpaper. Remember, a pattern or colour that looked great in a small piece in a shop may not look so great splashed all over a wall! When you are matching colours for paint, fabric or wallpaper, check each of them in both day and electric light. Colours can change remarkably under different lights and you may find that a colour you have carefully matched in shop lighting does not look at all the same in bright sunlight at home.

Strong colours and bold patterns tend to look best in large rooms. They can be overwhelming in a smaller area and should be avoided unless you are planning for a really dramatic effect. Be most adventurous in rooms like halls and bathrooms where you do not spend too much time at a stretch. Living-rooms and bedrooms should be relaxed and restful.

Decide what you want to be the dominating feature of your room—a dramatic colour, a beautiful carpet, stunning, patterned curtains or a group of your favourite pictures or ornaments—and subordinate the rest of your decoration to this. It is also important, even if you are planning to redecorate only one room, to take the décor of the rest of your house into account. The décor of one room should harmonize, not clash, with that of the next!

Above all, try to visualize the final effect of your new decorations before you come to any fixed decisions. By the time you actually finish, it's too late to change your mind!

Making a Start

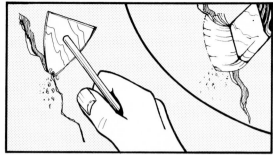

Careful and thorough preparation of all surfaces is essential before you start any redecorating job. If you paste new wallpaper over old, you may find that it soon starts coming away from the wall in patches, or blistering. Similarly, painting over flaking or dirty paint is a waste of time: the new paint will never adhere to the surface well enough to give a satisfactory finish. Time spent on preparation is never wasted.

Enlarge any small hairline cracks gently with a paint scraper. Brush out loose plaster or dust.

First, remove all the furniture and rugs that you can. Then, protect any that remain with heavy-duty dust sheets. You must cover the floor as well—especially if you have a fitted carpet. Next, tackle the old wallpaper. If it is vinyl, washable or varnished, score the surface with a wire brush so that water can penetrate more easily. Soak the wallpaper with warm water to which a squeeze of detergent has been added. Leave for twenty minutes and then strip it off with a wallpaper stripping knife. Wash and rinse the wall to ensure that all old wallpaper and paste have been removed.

Mix filler following manufacturer's instructions. Press into crack until it overflows.

Now start on the paintwork. All painted surfaces must be washed and rinsed. Use warm water and a detergent or, if the paint is very dirty, a weak solution of sugar-soap and water. Remove any patches of flaking or loose paint with a paint scraper. Then smooth with sandpaper. If you are going to paint the walls, check the plaster. Large holes or crumbling patches are better coped with by an experienced plasterer but you can repair any small cracks or holes by following the instructions (right). Uneven areas in the woodwork must also be made good: use the same method as for the plaster but smooth the filler on until it is flush against the surface and sand with glasspaper, not sandpaper.

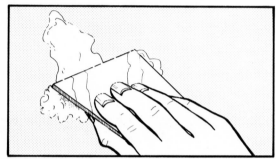

Smooth off excess filler with the paint scraper until the crack is flush to the surface.

When you are sure that all surfaces are as smooth and clean as you can get them, clear up any mess and debris that the preparatory work may have caused and start planning the sequence of your redecoration. Tackle the ceiling first, then the wood trim, then any walls that are to be painted. Leave the papering until last.

Our directions are for walls and woodwork in good structural condition. If you are decorating old, damaged rooms, we suggest you consult a comprehensive d-i-y book which includes a section on basic home repairs.

When the filler is nearly dry, rub gently with a damp sponge. When it is set hard, smooth with sandpaper.

Using Paint

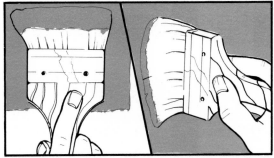

With a roller, apply paint in short strokes, spreading it evenly in all directions. When painting a ceiling, start near the window.

Work in square-metre sections with gloss paint. Always brush paint on in the same direction, working from top to bottom. Then spread the paint by brushing sideways with unloaded brush.

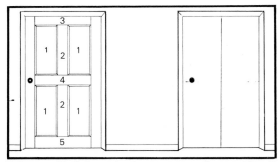

Apply emulsion paint in ragged strips, working from top to bottom. While still wet, brush over lightly with sideways strokes and an unloaded brush, to spread an even film.

Paint moulded doors in the sequence shown. After 5, continue down panels, working downwards. For flush doors, mentally divide the door into four equal squares and starting with a top square, work towards the centre line.

Walls or ceilings with uneven surfaces should be lined with lining paper first. This is applied in the same way as wallpaper— see page 14.

Ceilings are the most difficult part of the room to paint. Make sure you are working on a firm platform. A scaffolding board resting between two sturdy stepladders is best. You can use rollers on the ceiling, but we do not recommend them for walls because they never give as good a finish as painting with a brush. Never saturate or overload your roller—squeeze it out gently as you withdraw it from the tray. Before painting the main part of the ceiling, paint with a brush a strip of about 15cm all round the edges where the roller cannot reach. Select a lambswool roller for emulsion paint, a mohair one for gloss and a plastic roller only if the surface is very smooth.

There are so many new types of paint on the market that we cannot advise you on techniques for all of them here. It is wisest always to follow the manufacturer's instructions. The approximate area covered by different paints varies, as does the amount needed to get a good finish on different wall surfaces. For quantities, check with your supplier or follow the directions on the paint tin. As with wallpaper, be generous in the amount you buy. Colours vary quite radically between batches of paint manufactured at different times.

Remember that all bare timber surfaces must be primed with a suitable primer and undercoated before being painted. This applies to hardboard, chipboard and blockboard. When you paint any surface, it is preferable to apply more coats of Paint evenly and not too thickly than to try to get away with one thick coat!

The most widely available paints are still the traditional emulsion, gloss and semi-gloss or eggshell. Emulsion is suitable for most wall surfaces and is the *only* paint that should be used on newly-plastered walls. Gloss is the most practical paint for kitchens, bathrooms and all wood because it can be cleaned very easily. You can also use gloss when you want to achieve a particularly striking effect, as in *Up the Garden Path* (page 16), or to pick out a contrast with emulsion, as in our photograph on page 12. Eggshell can be used in the same circumstances as gloss. It is easier to apply but does not stand up to repeated cleaning nearly so well. Always keep your brushes clean. A clogged, stiff brush never gives good results. And never overload your brush. Dip only a third of it into the paint and squeeze out any excess paint by pressing the brush against the side of the paint tin.

When working with gloss paint, work quickly and try to finish the whole of a particular surface at one go. If the paint dries, there will be a hard edge which is almost impossible to blend in with the fresh paint when you start again. Be careful to apply both undercoat and topcoat in the same direction otherwise you will get a criss-cross effect instead of a smooth finish.

When painting wood, try to paint along the grain and use a cutting-in tool when you are painting the skirting board or the wall edges of doors and windows. The sloping bristles give a cleaner line than those of an ordinary brush. Use masking tape to protect woodwork when you are painting a wall near it in a different colour.

Painting with emulsion is a straight-forward job. A bad finish is usually caused by a faulty wall surface, not by the painting. If your wall is not smooth, we recommend that you paper rather than paint it. Or, you could try stippling. For this you need emulsion in three toning colours. Paint the wall in your basic colour. When that is dry, dab on the second colour with a sponge to give a speckled effect. Leave it to dry and then dab on the third colour, also with a sponge, in a more random pattern. Be careful not to overload the sponges. If you do, both the wall surface and you will be in a mess!

Disasters in painting are usually caused by haste—not preparing surfaces adequately, not priming bare timber or plaster surfaces, not leaving one coat to dry thoroughly before applying the next. Painting needs patience. Don't take short cuts, or all your work may be wasted.

In this drawing-room, the moulding on the wall panels has been picked out in gloss as a subtle contrast to the emulsion finish for the rest of the wall.

Using Wallpaper

Papering is one of the most pleasant decorating jobs and surprisingly easy once you know how. Check that your wall surface is reasonably smooth. If it is pitted or very uneven, line it first with heavy-duty lining paper. This should be pasted up on the wall *horizontally,* the edges of each piece butted-up tightly.

Steer clear of the more exotic wallpapers, like flock, silk or cork, which are not easy to hang and could mean an expensive disaster! Thin wallpapers, though usually cheap, are not recommended either. They are difficult to handle and tear easily. Choose medium-weight wallpapers and, unless you have done a fair amount of paperhanging before, avoid obtrusive patterns which require very accurate matching. Note that vinyl papers need a special paste, unless they are ready-pasted (in which case, follow the manufacturer's instructions). Always check that the wallpaper you buy is ready-trimmed. If not, ask your supplier to trim it for you.

An experienced supplier will always advise on the amount of paper needed, but it is as well to learn how to estimate for standard-width wallpaper. You calculate in exactly the same way for a non-standard paper or for fabric, but remember to adjust the width measurement.

Standard wallpaper rolls are 530mm wide and 10.5m long. Measure all round your room, including door and window space. Divide this measurement by the wallpaper width, that is 530mm. The result equals the number of cut lengths you will need plus one for any number 'left over'. Now measure the height of your room. Each length must equal this height plus an extra 10cm to allow for a 5cm overlap at the top and bottom of the walls. Now calculate how many full lengths you can get out of a standard roll. There will be wastage but odd pieces can often be used above or below windows.

Always allow extra for pattern matching and be generous in your estimating. Batches of wallpaper ordered at different times often do not colour-match exactly. Worse still, patterns go out of production and your whole décor can be ruined for want of half a roll or less.

Painted and papered walls have been mixed in this elegant hall. This serves to break up large surfaces, which are monotonous if they are all in one colour or pattern.

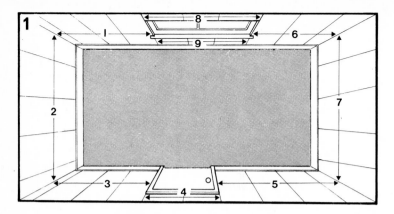

1

Check that you have the necessary equipment* before you start papering (see page 7). Paper the room in the sequence shown, working away from the windows towards the door.

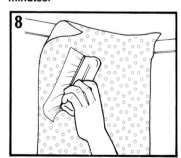

2

In a room with a prominent chimney breast where patterned paper is to be used, hang the first length centrally over the chimney breast.

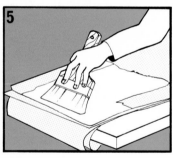

3

Using a plumb line, mark a true vertical, the width of one wallpaper strip away from the window.

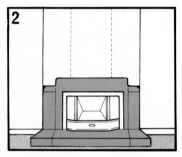

4

Cut the first six lengths. Be careful to match the pattern before you cut.

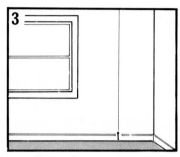

5

Paste first length, starting at top centre and covering edges well. Allow paste to penetrate paper for 5 minutes.

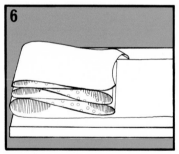

6

Keeping pasted surfaces together, fold paper as shown. Paste next length and leave to soak.

7

Allowing 5cm overlap at both top and bottom, slide paper into position against vertical line.

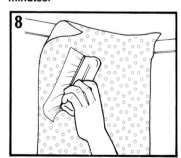

8

Using paperhanging brush and working from the top centre outwards, smooth paper with even pressure.

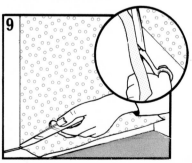

9

Using back of scissors, press in trim lines at top and bottom. Ease paper from wall, trim and smooth back into place.

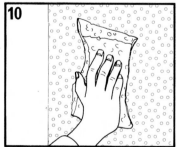

10

Ensure that there are no air bubbles by going over the surface with a sponge. Work from the centre outwards.

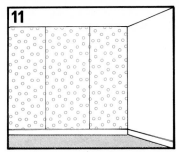

11

Continue pasting lengths into position, ensuring that adjoining lengths butt-up closely. Always *slide* paper into position.

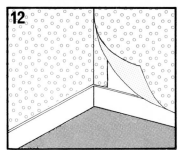

12

Don't carry paper round corners. Trim up corner length allowing 5cm overlap. Paste off-cut over overlap.

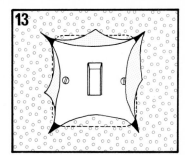

13

For square electrical switches, trim paper to corners as shown. Smooth around edges when trimmed.

14

For round switches, trim by cutting a series of triangles. Cut off triangles round fitting. Smooth into place.

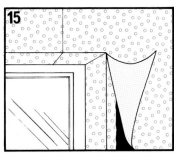

15

For a recessed window or alcove, first paper recess allowing 5cm overlap. Paste next length over overlap, trimming at recess edge.

16

When hanging paper, check for true verticals by hanging a plumb line at every corner.

Using Fabric

Fabric-covered walls are fun and unusual and you'll see them in several of our projects. Estimate the amount needed in the same way as for wallpaper (see page 12), but check the width of the fabric (this varies considerably) and always allow for pattern-matching. When you come to choose your fabric, remember certain basic dos and don'ts.

Choose a fairly heavy fabric. A light fabric will not hang as flat and may let light through. You don't want to see your wall through its covering! Choose furnishing rather than dress fabric, unless we specifically recommend the latter (as in *Try a Tent* page 72). Furnishing fabric tends to be more economical because it is made in greater widths and any left over can be used for cushions or even small curtains. Check that the fabric does not fray too easily, otherwise it can be difficult to work with and won't produce a neat finish. Try to buy fabric that is guaranteed against fading—sunlight can alter colours

remarkably quickly. Don't buy a fabric with too loose a weave. It will stretch and become distorted as you hang it and, if you glue it (as in our project *Hide a Hole,* page 80), you risk a patchy finish where the glue saturates the cloth. Don't forget that all fabric should be sewn or hung so that the weave runs in the same direction—parallel to the selvedges. Don't choose very light colours: they're likely to stain round light switches and doors and, once up, the fabric cannot easily be cleaned.

Certain furnishing fabrics like hessian and felt can be applied directly to the walls in the same way as wallpaper. But you must ensure that you are using a suitable paste and that, instead of butting-up the edges of each length as for wallpaper, you overlap them and then trim when the paste is dry. (See our directions for felt in *Bring Down the Ceiling,* page 60.) For hanging felt you will need help, as it's extremely heavy to handle.

Mini Doors

The door wastes a lot of space in a small room or landing because it must be allowed sufficient clearance to open fully. If you are pushed for space, why not saw your door vertically in two? It will look attractive and original, and you will be surprised at the space saved. This treatment is best for moulded doors, the mouldings of which can be picked out in a contrasting colour. It is not suitable for flush doors because these are usually hollow inside. (For some ideas on flush doors, see page 92.)

YOU WILL NEED:
4 door knobs
4 65mm brass butt hinges
Tenon saw
Chisel
Screwdriver · Screws
Rigid rule
Pencil
10 × 35mm batten the length
   of door
Sandpaper
Gloss paint in 2 colours
Paint brushes
Plastic wood and/or putty

Remove door from frame. Unscrew hinges. Remove existing handles and locks.

Draw a line down the centre of the door. Saw along line. Sand sawn edges to smooth finish.

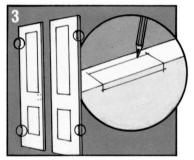

Measure position of old hinges. On new door mark corresponding position for new hinges.

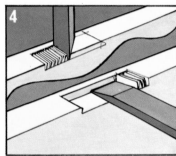

Chisel cut-outs where marked so that new hinges can be inserted.

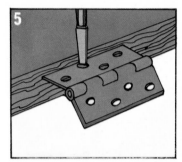

Screw hinges loosely into place. Position doors against frame. Mark and chisel cut-outs on frame for new hinges.

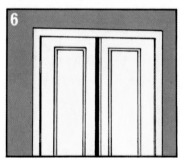

Screw doors loosely into frame to check for easy action. You'll see a gap between doors at this stage.

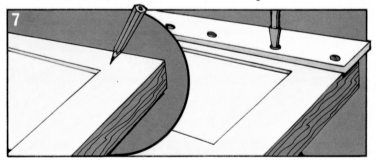

Take doors down and remove hinges. To cover gap, on one door mark a straight line, 2cm from edge, and screw batten along line allowing a 2cm overlap at door edge.

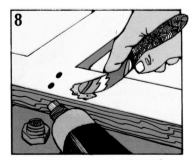

Fill holes on frame and doors from handles, locks, etc with putty (for larger holes), or plastic wood. Sand when dry.

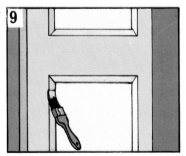

Paint doors in main gloss shade. When dry, paint mouldings in contrast.

Attach hinges and re-hang doors. Attach knobs to both sides at centre of doors.

Hidden Heat

Although essential, radiators are often ugly and space-consuming, especially in a narrow hallway. This radiator has been covered with a decorative grille and the framework provides an attractive shelf for ornaments or tropical plants. Our instructions are for a finished size of 122cm high × 107cm wide × 10cm deep, measurements which you may have to adjust to suit your own radiators. Remember when measuring them to leave space for side valves and to allow 15.25cm extra on the overall width and 7.5cm extra on the overall height for air circulation. You can paint the frame either to blend or to contrast with your walls.

YOU WILL NEED:
4.5m plywood, 2.5 × 10cm
5m wooden battening,
   35 × 25mm
4 small L-brackets plus
   screws
2 small T-brackets plus
   screws
Drill · Rawlplugs · Wood glue
Screws · Screwdriver · Hammer
Coppered hardboard pins
Panelaire,* 1070 × 1220mm
   (see box 11)
4 medium picture brackets
4 medium spring clips plus
   screws
Saw · Mitre box
Primer · Undercoat
Heatproof gloss paint
Paint brushes
*See list of suppliers on page 94

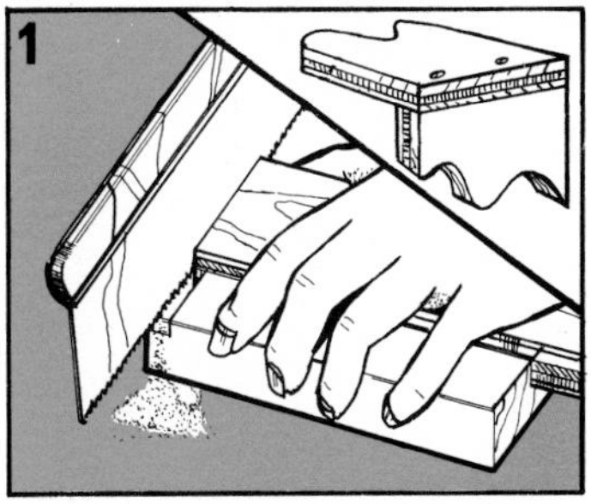

To make outer frame, saw plywood into four pieces, two of 122cm and two of 107cm. Glue and screw together.

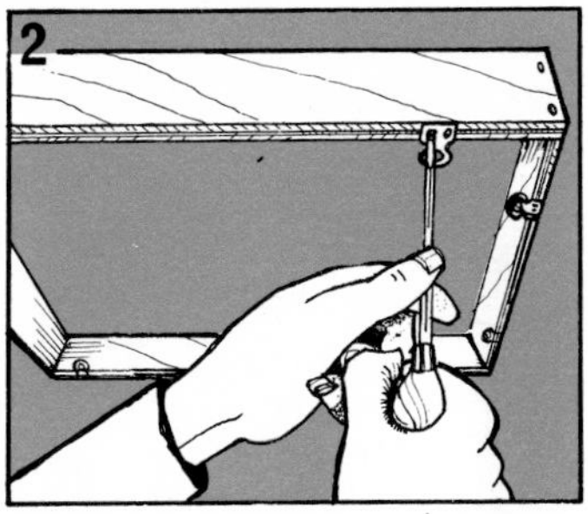

Screw picture brackets to back of frame, 20cm from top and bottom corners.

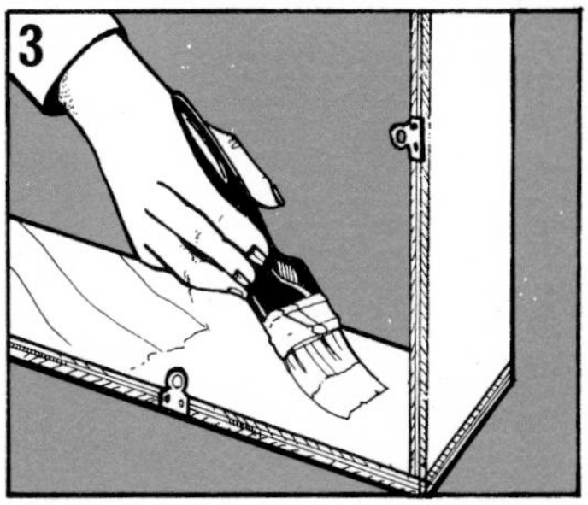

Prime, undercoat and paint frame with one coat of gloss. Leave to dry.

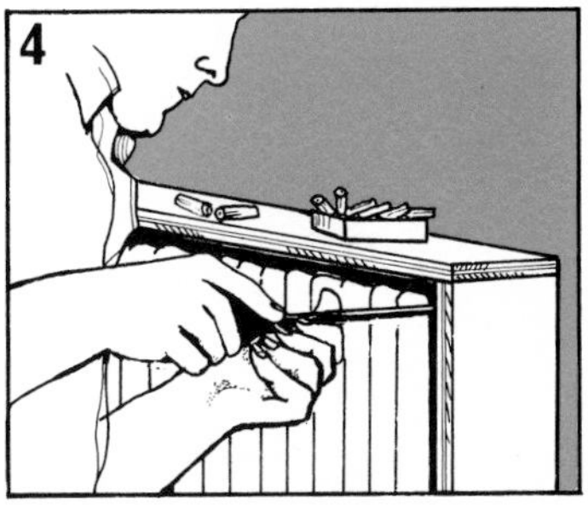

Using rawlplugs and drill (see page 43) screw frame to wall in position over radiator through picture brackets.

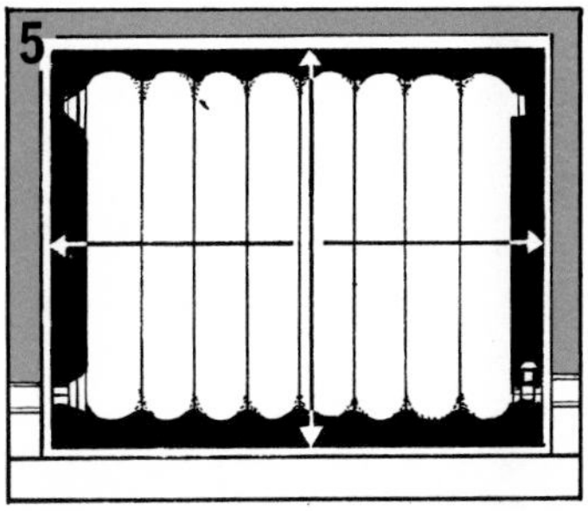

Measure interior of frame. Using mitre box to form 45° angles at each end, saw two battens to frame height, two to width.

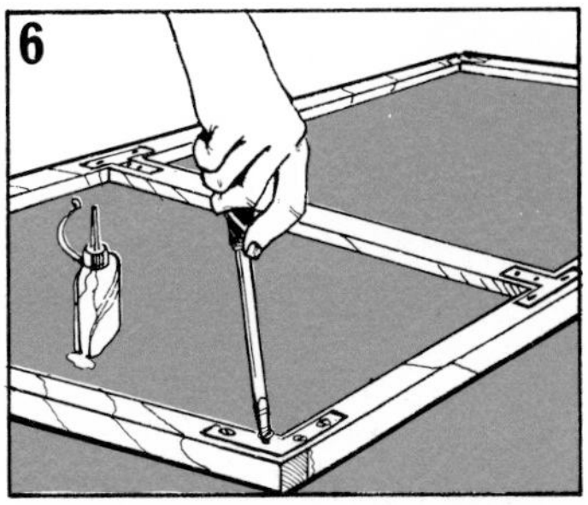

Glue and screw battens together, using L-brackets at corners. Saw a cross batten to size, glue and screw in place with T-brackets.

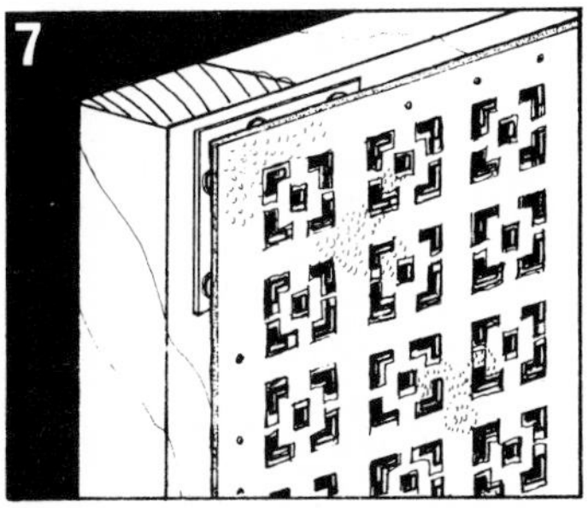

Cut Panelaire 1.25cm narrower and 1.25cm shorter than batten frame. Using pins, nail to back of frame.

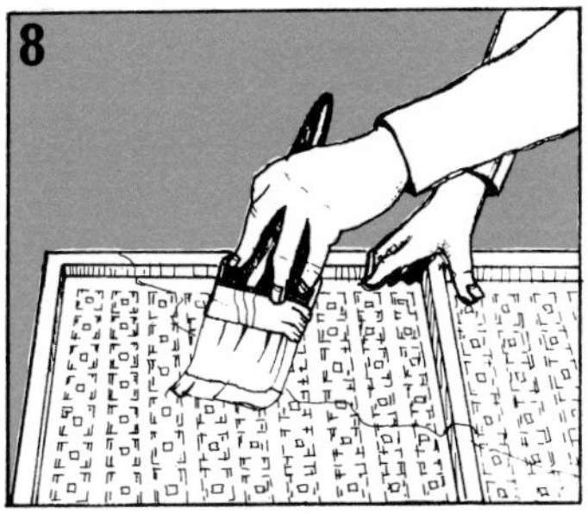

Prime, undercoat, then paint grille with one coat of gloss. Do not overload brush while painting. Leave to dry between coats.

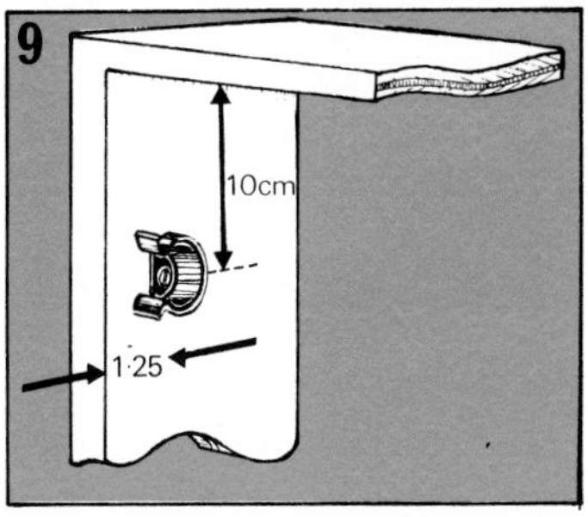

On outer frame, screw base of spring clips 1.25cm from edge and 10cm from top and bottom at each side.

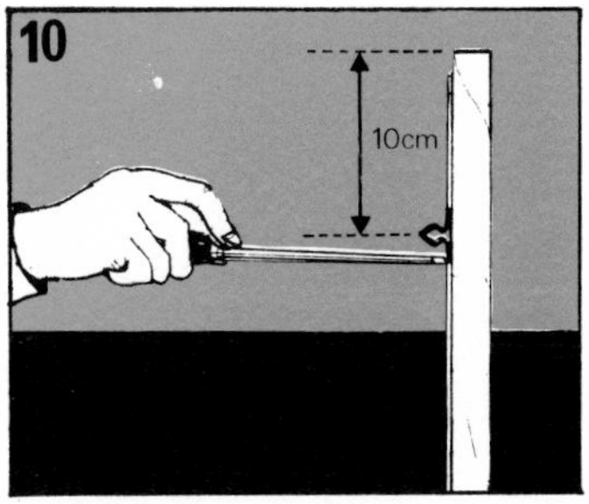

On grille frame, screw top of spring clips to back, 10cm from top and bottom. Clip grille into place.

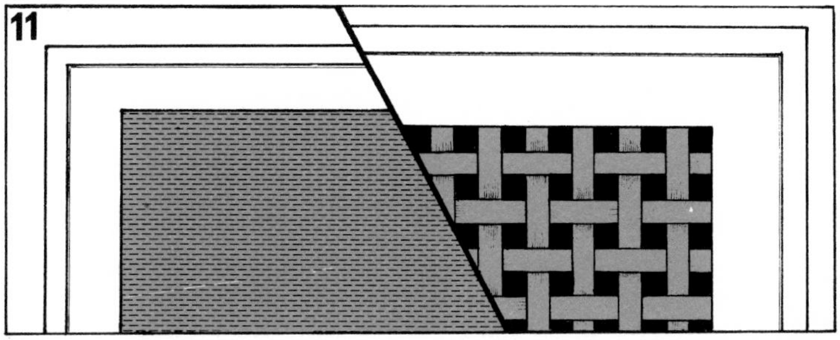

You can use chicken wire or woven cane in place of the Panelaire. Paint the wire gold to make it look like an expensive brass grille. The cane can be painted to match your décor or left in its natural colour.

Country Kitchen

Here we show you a town-house kitchen that makes you look forward to country cooking. The floor is covered with ceramic tiles– page 22 shows you how to lay them— and the walls are clad in tongued-and-grooved board 'panelling'. This can be ordered through your d-i-y shop or bought direct from a timber merchant. It is commonly sold in widths of 100mm. This width includes the tongue so that, in position, each board covers a width of 85mm. Estimate as for wallpaper (see page 13). You will need sufficient battening to place at 45cm intervals horizontally across each wall. You will also need enough of the quadrant to go along the floor and tops of walls, and around doors and windows.

Don't take chances with the electricity. Turn off at the mains as directed or, if you have old wiring, consult your local Electricity Board, or an experienced electrician.

YOU WILL NEED:
Tongued and grooved boards
50 × 25mm battens
20mm quadrant wood
  moulding
Saw · Hammer
Oval wire nails
Screwdriver
Drill · Rawlplugs · Screws
Padsaw · Putty
Countersink
Electrical tape
Tenon saw · Mitre box
Rigid rule · Plane
Clear polyurethane varnish
Paint brush

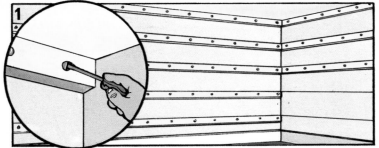

1. Measure width of walls. Saw battens to size. Using drill and rawlplugs (see page 43), screw batten along ceiling and at 45cm intervals across walls. Use skirting board as base batten.

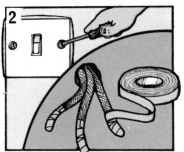

2. Switch off electricity supply at mains. Remove electric fittings. Tape wires separately and securely.

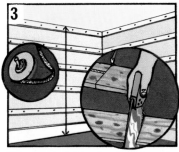

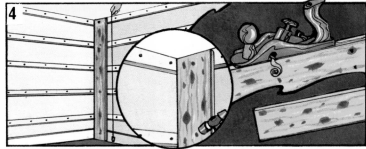

3. Measure height of walls, floor to ceiling. Saw boards to size.

4. Start at corner and using plumb line to ensure true vertical position, nail first board, grooved edge flush to corner, to battens at centre. Plane tongued edge off second board.

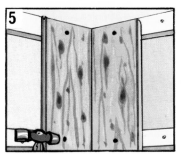

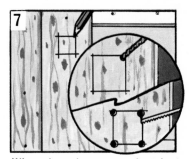

5. Butt up second board to first at corner. Using plumb line to ensure true vertical, nail to battens.

6. Tapping gently but firmly with hammer so that boards fit together *tightly*, continue nailing round wall.

7. When board covers electrical outlet, mark position of outlet on board. Using drill and padsaw cut a 2.5cm-square hole at mark.

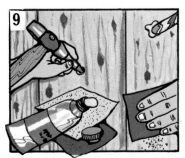

8. Nail cut board into position. Pull electrical wires through hole. Reconnect wires to fitting, screw fitting on to board.

9. When all boards are in place, sink nails using countersink and hammer. Stop up holes with putty. Sand when dry.

10. Measure around top and bottom of walls and windows and along top of door. Measure up corners and sides of door and window.

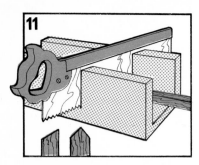

11 Using mitre box, saw quadrant to these measures: horizontal quadrant to have 45° at each end; vertical quadrant to have double 45° angles.

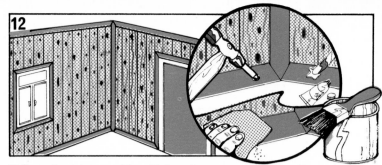

12 Nail quadrant into position. Sink and stop up nail holes. Sand when dry. Ensuring wall surface is clean and smooth, paint with one coat of polyurethane varnish. Leave to dry. Switch on electricity at mains.

Ceramic Floor

Ceramic floors are among the most practical and attractive floor surfaces. Do not use ceramic tiles, however, if your floor is uneven or not firmly supported. They are best used on level *concrete* floors where they will give many years of service.

YOU WILL NEED:
Floor-tile adhesive
Trowel
Spacer pegs
Tile cutter
Carborundum stone
Grout
Squeegee
155mm ceramic floor tiles
Battens

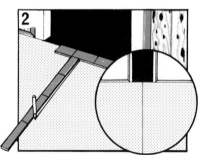

1 Unless door allows for an extra 15mm of floor at the bottom, remove door.

2 Mark line across floor at 90° angle to centre of door opening.

3 Measure off widths of 155mm along line, starting at door.

4 Nail batten to floor at an accurate 90° angle to marked line. Nail where last full tile-width marked.

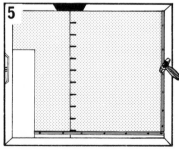

5 Nail second batten near wall at an accurate 90° angle to first. If room irregular, nail corresponding batten opposite.

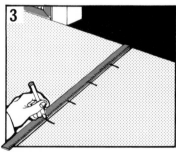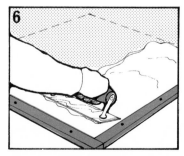

6 Starting at corner formed by two battens, and using trowel, spread adhesive thickly over 1 square metre of floor.

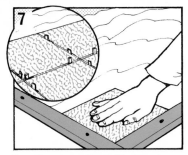

Gently press first tile in place. Using spacer pegs, continue to tile area covered by adhesive.

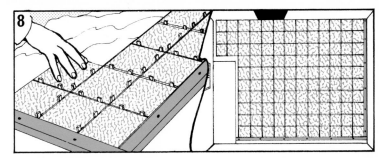

Repeat steps 5 and 6, spreading adhesive and laying tiles until the area within the battens is completely covered.

Measure tiles, one by one, for fitting at edges. Remember to allow 1.5mm extra for spacer pegs.

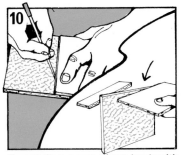

To cut tiles, score along back with tile cutter. Strike tile at score line against edge of another tile.

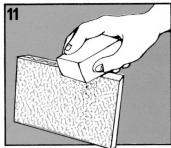

Smooth cut edge of tile with carborundum stone.

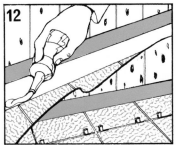

Cover floor at edge with adhesive. Using spacer pegs, place tiles with cut edges flush to wall.

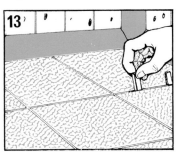

Leave tiles to dry for a minimum of 24 hours. Remove spacer pegs.

If door removed, check amount necessary to allow for opening over tile thickness. Plane off excess. Sand. Replace door.

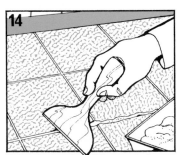

Using squeegee, fill gaps between tiles with grout, grouting in areas of 1 square metre.

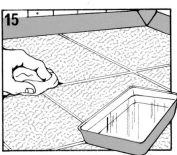

As grout over each area starts to set, clean off excess with damp cloth. Leave to dry.

Easy Seat

If you have a long, narrow room, make use of your wall space. Instead of buying bulky chairs and sofas, construct a luxurious wall-attached seating area. The seating in our picture is made up of a succession of basic box units. Covered with foam rubber pads and piled high with scatter cushions, these units are comfortable and practical. Being hollow, they provide valuable storage space, invaluable for last-minute tidying-up when unexpected guests arrive!

YOU WILL NEED:
2 sheets 12.5mm chipboard, 91 × 30cm
3 sheets 12.5mm chipboard, 73.5 × 30cm
1 sheet 12.5mm chipboard, 91 × 76cm
4 large picture brackets
Rawlplugs · Drill
Screwdriver · Screws
1.6m material, 86cm wide
Upholstery tacks
Hammer
95cm fringing, 30cm deep
Staple gun and staples

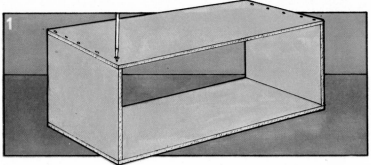

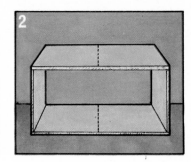

Screw four pieces of chipboard together to form a hollow box measuring 91 × 76 × 30cm. Screw securely at the corners and at 10cm intervals along the joints.

Mark line at the centre across the top and bottom of box as guide for position of centre support.

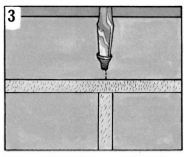

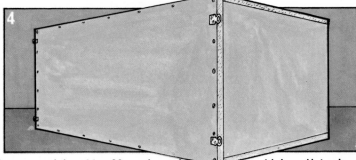

For centre support, insert the extra 73.5 × 30cm sheet of chipboard in marked position. Screw into place at 10cm intervals.

Screw remaining 91 × 30cm piece of chipboard into place as back of box. At each side, screw two picture brackets 5cm from top and bottom.

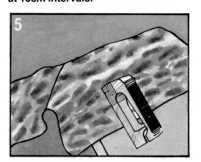

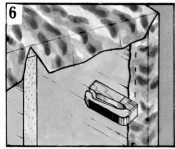

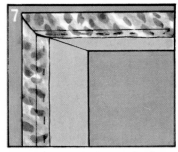

To cover box with fabric, first tilt on one side. With a 5cm overlap each side, staple one end of material along base, 5cm from edge.

Fold overlap to inside of box and staple down the raw edges of material. Trim as shown near centre support.

At corners, mitre the overlap for a neat finish.

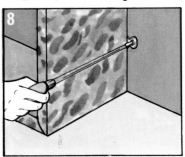

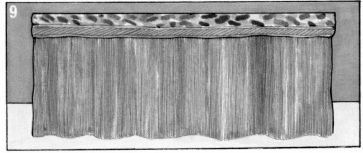

Select position for box against wall. Through bracket holes, drill and plug wall. Screw box into place.

Turning in 2cm at each end of fringe, attach fringe to front of box using upholstery tacks. Make similar boxes until you have a bench of the required length.

Instant Elegance

If you favour 18th-century elegance, you can transform a modern room by the application of decorative carvings. A wide range of these can be bought through most d-i-y shops or direct from the manufacturers. Our illustration features 'Softwood Carvings' which are supplied as individual pieces or as complete designs and a Roman blind, which we show you how to make on page 28. If you are a beginner, we recommend you start by applying the complete designs. Once you have had practice, work out your own. In this sitting-room, the wall area behind the frieze and door have been painted in contrasting colours to highlight the decorations. Measure around your walls to establish the amount of moulding and frieze you will need. Most door designs are supplied with their component parts for standard doors of 198 × 76cm. Make sure your door and wall surfaces are clean and smooth before applying the carvings.

YOU WILL NEED:
Purchased frieze and door
 carvings*
Straight decorative moulding
 to go twice round room
White emulsion · Gloss paint
Paint brushes · Spirit level
Veneer (panel) pins
Hammer
PVC glue
Sandpaper
Sealing tape

*See list of suppliers on
 page 94

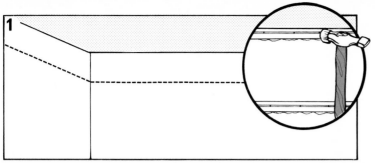

1

For frieze: mark off a continuous line around walls 17cm below ceiling level. Glue and pin, with veneer pins, straight moulding along line. Glue and pin a parallel strip butted up to ceiling. Paint strips and frieze area with one coat emulsion.

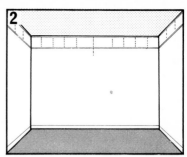

2

Mark off centre point on each wall in frieze area. Working from this point, mark off widths of design repeat.

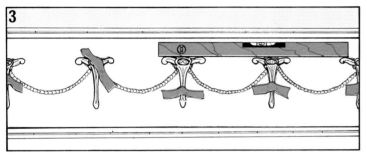

3

Using sealing tape, tape frieze into position along centre of frieze area, checking frequently with spirit level to ensure straightness. Glue and pin frieze design to wall.

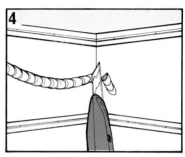

4

If design needs to be cut at corners, use a trimming knife and sand edges smooth before fixing.

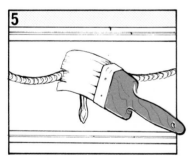

5

Paint mouldings, frieze and wall area with two coats of emulsion thinly applied.

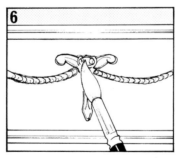

6

For a greater contrast, the carvings can be picked out in gloss. Prime them first with one coat of emulsion.

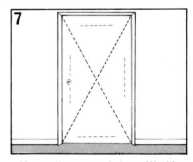

7

Mark off centre of door. Working from centre, mark off maximum height and width of door carving.

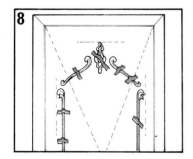

8

Starting at top centre of design, apply it to door with sealing tape.

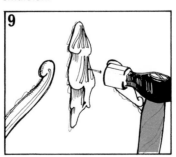

9

Using glue and pins, affix design to door.

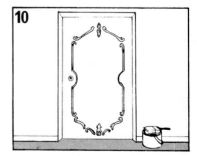

10

Prime moulding with one coat of emulsion. When dry, paint with one coat of gloss thinly applied.

Let the Sunshine In

Roman blinds are an attractive and economic alternative to curtains—they take far less material. Choose a fairly heavy-quality cotton. If it is too flimsy the blinds will not fold or hang so well. Measure the height and width of your window, including the frame. Buy enough of the main shade to cover this area, minus 30cm. Buy enough of the trimming to make two strips the full length of your window and 18cm wide, plus one strip to the full width of the window and 20cm long. You need enough lining to cover the entire window area. If your windows are less than 91cm in width we recommend that you make plain rather than trimmed blinds.

YOU WILL NEED:
2 shades of cotton fabric
Matching sewing thread
Curtain lining
1 25 × 25mm wooden batten to width of window
1 25 × 6mm wooden batten for every 30cm of window height
2 small brass rings
Small screw eyes
Small brass cleat
Saw · Drill
Pencil · Rigid rule
Screwdriver · Screws
1 1.25cm mild steel rod, 2.5cm less than width of window in length
Medium-weight nylon cord, 5 times height and once width of window plus knotting length
Staple gun · Staples

1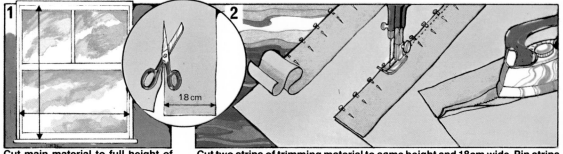

Cut main material to full height of window frame and full width minus 30cm.

2

Cut two strips of trimming material to same height and 18cm wide. Pin strips to sides of material. Join main material and trimming together, by machining a 1.5cm seam on each side.

3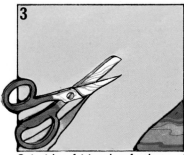

Cut strip of trimming for base of blind to full width of blind and 20cm in depth.

4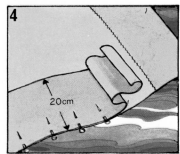

Pin base to blind. Machine 1.5cm seam. Press.

5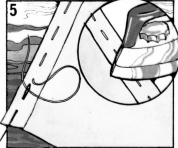

Cut lining to same width as blind, but 4cm shorter. Tack and press 2cm turn-in along sides.

6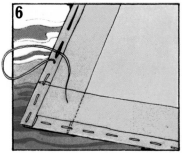

Tack and press 1.5cm turn-in along sides and bottom of blind.

7

Matching lining and material at top edges, pin wrong sides together, (bottom of lining will be 4cm shorter than blind).

8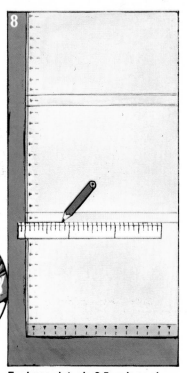

For base slot, pin 2.5cm hem along bottom of blind. Press. Lay blind flat. Mark off 30cm sections on lining.

9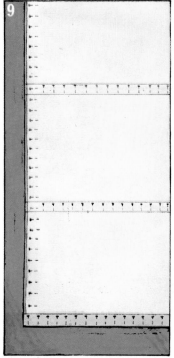

Pencil in lines 4.5cm away from first lines to make slots. Pin at 2.5cm intervals between lines.

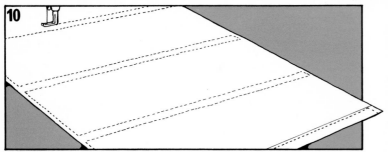

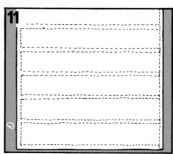

To make remaining slots, machine along edge of hem, following marked pencil lines as shown, in one continuous line.

Machine along edge with closed ends, as shown above. Remove pins and tacking.

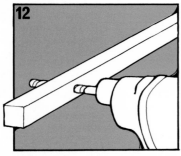

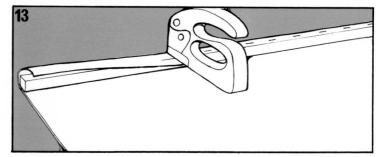

Drill two holes 7.5cm in from ends of 25 × 25mm batten. If window is over 122cm wide, drill hole at centre too.

Lay blind flat, lining up. Place batten across blind 6cm from top. Fold top of blind over batten. Staple blind to batten, inserting staples as close together as possible, in a straight line.

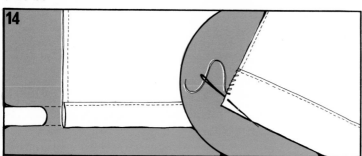

Slide mild steel rod into hem of blind. Hand-sew over opening to close after insertion.

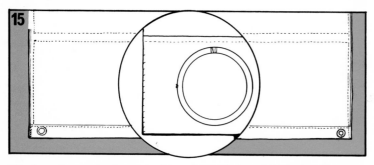

Hand-sew brass ring to edge of hem 2.5cm in from blind edge. Repeat at opposite corner, as shown.

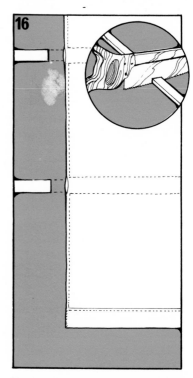

For each slot, saw 25 × 6mm battens, each 1.25cm shorter than width of blind. Slide battens into slots.

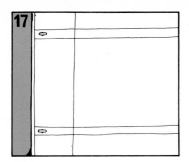

17

With lining facing, fix screw eyes into battens, 2.5cm from edges of blind.

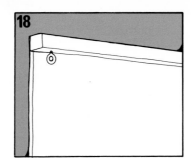

18

Fix screw eyes into base of top batten, as shown, 2.5cm from edges.

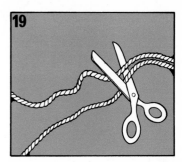

19

Cut two lengths of cord: A, the width and twice the height of blind, and B, twice the height of blind, plus knot allowance.

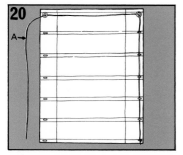

20

Take A: tie end to brass ring, as shown, at bottom right-hand corner. Thread through rings up one side and across top of blind.

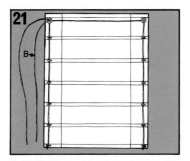

21

Take B: tie end to ring at opposite corner, but thread up one side of blind only, as shown.

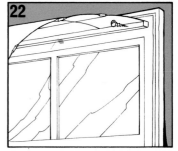

22

Lift blind. Through holes in top batten of blind, screw it to edge of top window frame, as shown.

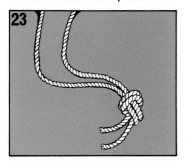

23

Check that cords are equal in length. Tie ends together to form loop.

24

Screw cleat to side of window frame, 4cm from base.

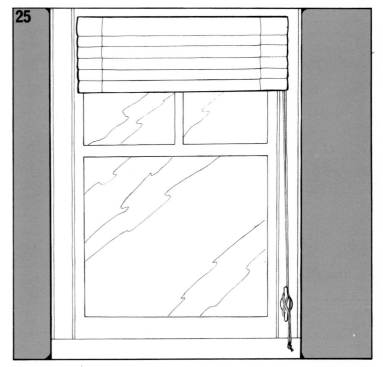

25

Pull blind to maximum height and hold at this position by wrapping cords round cleat. Leave blind pulled up for 24 hours to allow folds to set.

Floor Show

Although some very attractive patterned vinyl tiles are available, you can create a more distinctive floor by using plain colours in a bold design. Our floor, suitable for a more or less square room, is in white, blue and green tiles. The design covers an area of 3 square metres but can easily be adapted for larger areas—simply fill in round the edges with white tiles.

N.B. You will need a hardboard base (see page 46 for laying instructions) unless your floor is of well-levelled concrete.

YOU WILL NEED:
250 × 250mm self-adhesive
  vinyl floor tiles:
    36 white; 44 light blue; 24
    dark blue; 24 light green;
    16 dark green
Hardboard to cover floor area
Coppered hardboard pins
Hammer
Plastic wood
Sandpaper
Felt-tip pen
Rigid rule
Stanley knife
Plastic tile sealer

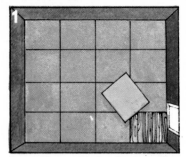

1 Cover floor with hardboard. (See page 46, but do not prime and paint hardboard.)

2 Mark off centre point of all four walls. Join marks with two lines to establish centre of room.

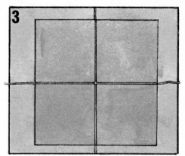

3 Following manufacturer's instructions, lay and stick light blue tiles at centre. Butt-up edges closely.

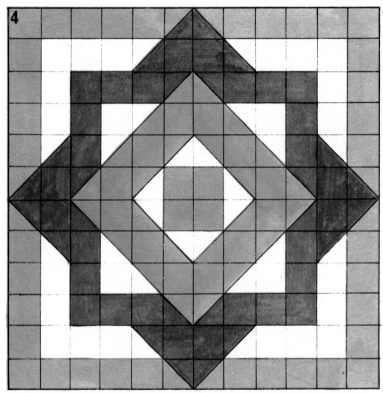

4 If your room is square follow this grid, remembering that one square in the diagram equals one tile.

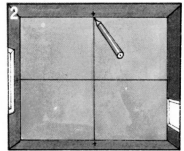

5 Following design, work in a circle from centre tiles outwards.

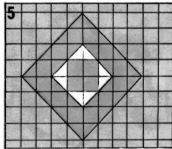

6 Cut triangular tile accurately using rule and Stanley knife.

7 When floor is completed, seal with plastic sealer.

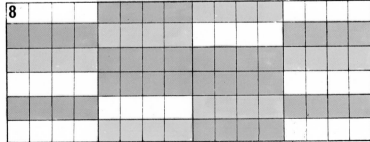

8 Here is another design, suitable for a long room. Work from the centre tiles as in previous design. Attractive alternative colours could be black, tan and orange.

Circus Top

It's not easy to get away from a box-like feeling in a small, square room, but one way to do it is to focus attention on the ceiling. Here we show a dining-room decorated in black and white evenly striped wallpaper with matching ceiling. The idea is equally effective in a bathroom, lavatory or square entrance hall. (To estimate the amount of wallpaper needed for the walls and ceiling, see the wallpaper section, page 13.) You will need enough braid to surround the room, to cross the ceiling twice, and to cover each corner from floor to ceiling; and enough bobbled braid to go twice round the room.

YOU WILL NEED:
Black-and-white-striped
 wallpaper
Paste brush
Wallpaper paste
Steel rule
Stanley knife
Pencil
Saucer, 15cm in diameter
5cm-wide black braid
2.5cm-wide bobbled braid
 (black, or black and white)
Rubber-based adhesive

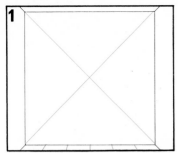

1 Draw diagonal lines across ceiling. Starting at corner, mark off wallpaper widths along edge of ceiling.

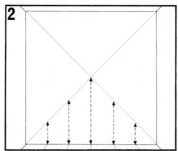

2 Measure from marks to lines as shown. Cut wallpaper into lengths of these measurements, plus 5cm on each length.

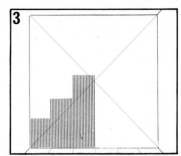

3 Working in 'triangles', position wallpaper as shown. Starting at corner, paste into place.

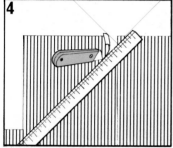

4 Starting at centre, trim excess, using rule and Stanley knife.

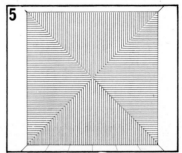

5 Repeat until each 'triangle' of ceiling is covered.

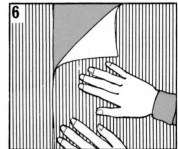

6 Paper rest of the room. For instructions see page 14.

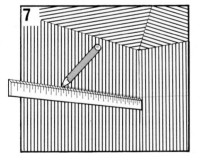

7 Draw a line 22cm below ceiling all round room.

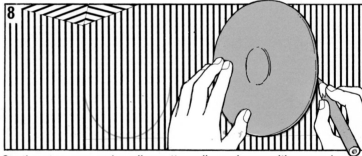

8 Starting at corner, mark scallop pattern all round room with saucer, leaving 8cm between scallops. Join with straight line.

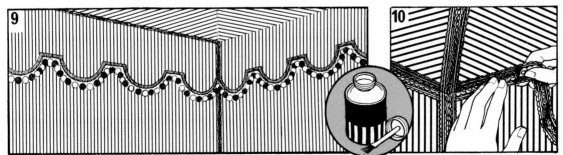

9 Using fabric adhesive, stick plain braid diagonally across ceiling to cover paper joins. Then stick it along top of walls and down all corners to floor. Stick bobbled braid along marked border all round room.

10 Take care to mitre braid at corners so that it is not bulky.

Soft Touch

Material such as cotton, softly gathered, can hide all the blemishes in a room that has uneven or difficult wall surfaces. Here it is used in a dining-room, but it is equally suitable for bedrooms. For the material: measure the height of your walls from floor to ceiling; measure the width of your walls and double it, to allow for gathers. Allow an extra 10cm for each length, and remember to allow for pattern matching. For the battens and tubes: measure along the top and bottom of each wall, the top and bottom of each window and along the top of each door. You will need battens cut to size for each individual measurement. Ask your supplier to cut the brass tubes to the required lengths.

YOU WILL NEED:
Material (see left)
Matching sewing thread
50 × 25mm wooden battens
10mm brass case tubes
2 face-fix sockets (with screws), per cut length of tube
Rawlplugs
Screws
Drill
Screwdriver
Saw
Cup-hooks large enough to carry case tubes

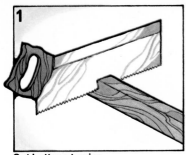

Cut battens to size.

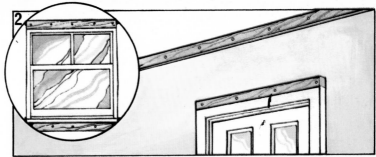

Using drill, plug and screw battens to top and bottom of walls, over doors, and above and below windows, as shown.

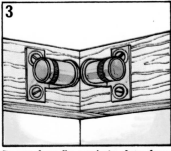

Screw face-fix sockets 4cm from batten ends at top and bottom corners. Repeat with door and window battens.

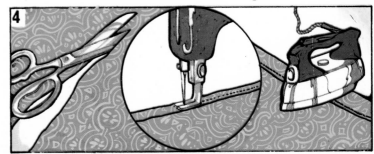

Cut material into panels the height of walls plus 10cm. Allow double fullness for each wall area. Sew a 1.5cm hem along selvedges. Press.

Machine 1.5cm hem along top and bottom of each panel to prevent fraying. Press. Tack another hem, considerably deeper, along top and bottom of each panel. Machine two rows for rod insertion, (a) along edge of hem, (b) 2.5cm away from edge. Press.

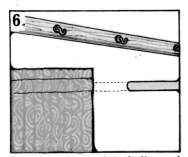

Screw cup-hooks into battens at top of walls, at about 60cm intervals. Slide rods into top and bottom of panels.

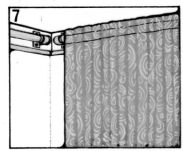

Fix rods in sockets at top of walls, doors and windows, supporting rods on cup-hooks. Fix rods below windows.

Attach rods at wall base, spread material evenly. Cut 12cm slits over light switches; turn in 6mm around slit. Hand-sew into place.

Two in One

If a room has to serve a dual function don't always try to disguise the fact. Accentuate the difference with a screen of living plants. If you haven't got green fingers, you could always wire plastic flowers or exotic fruits and vegetables on to poles. Here we show you a kitchen/dining-room, but the idea would look equally good in a bedsitter. Don't make your screen too large. A third of the way across the room is ample. These measurements are for a base of 137cm in length × 20cm deep × 15cm in height. Adjust the length to suit yourself but keep to the other dimensions. The poles must be 4cm in diameter, each to the height of room, less 5cm.

YOU WILL NEED:
6m whitewood, 25 × 150mm
5 whitewood poles
Saw
Plastic wood and/or filler
Sandpaper
Primer · Undercoat · Gloss paint
25mm and 50mm paint brushes
5 dowel screws
Screws
Drill
Rawlplugs · Screws
Plumb line
Decorative gravel or marble chippings
Pot plants

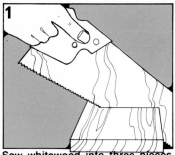

1 Saw whitewood into three pieces (base and side panels) 137cm long, and two pieces 20cm long (box ends).

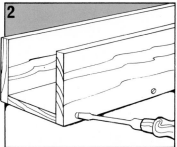

2 Screw side and end panels to base. Stop up holes with plastic wood or filler. Sand when dry.

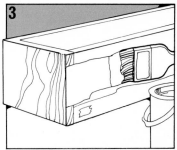

3 Prime base, inside and out. When dry, paint with undercoat and a coat of gloss.

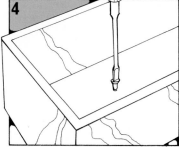

4 Place base in position. If on wooden floor, screw down. Otherwise leave free-standing.

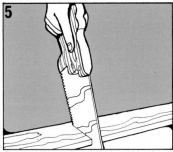

5 Saw whitewood piece 137cm long for ceiling support.

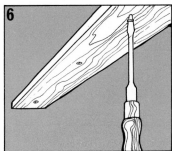

6 Ensure (with plumb line) that support is directly above base. Using drill and rawlplugs, screw into place.

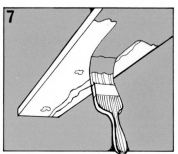

7 Stop up holes with plastic wood. Sand. Prime and paint support, to match ceiling. Leave to dry.

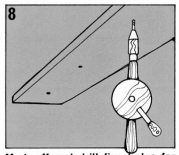

8 Mark off and drill five holes for screws at 30.5cm intervals on support.

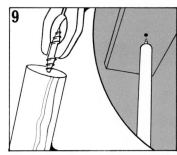

9 Screw dowel screws into one end of each pole. Screw poles into prepared holes in ceiling support.

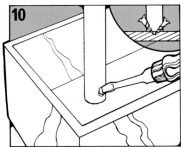

10 Ensuring poles are vertical, screw into base. The protruding screws will be hidden by gravel.

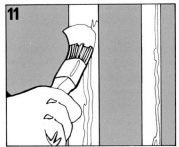

11 Prime, and paint poles with undercoat and one coat of gloss.

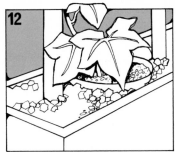

12 Place pot plants at base of poles. Fill base with decorative gravel.

Light Reflections

In this dining-room, part of one wall has been covered with mottled glass panels. You can get much the same effect using Perspex panels and painting your own design on the back, to colours of your choice. The shiny surface will not only help to give an illusion of greater space to your room but will be a totally unique wall surface, designed and executed by you. Remember that it may be possible to see the wall through the design, so its colour should blend with your painted Perspex. Our instructions show you how to cover one centre wall. Measure its surface area and divide it into equal panels of not less than 60cm square. If your wall doesn't divide equally, set trimmed panels at bottom of wall. Order panels already cut to size. Buy enough battening to go along the top, bottom and sides of walls and across the wall at lower edge of each row of panels.

YOU WILL NEED:
Wooden battens, 25 × 50mm
Woodscrews
Rawlplugs · Drill
Saw
Screwdriver
Clear Perspex panels*
Mirror screws with domed heads
Primer · Emulsion paint
Paint brush
Aerosol cans of paint (gloss or emulsion) in 2 shades of same colour

*See list of suppliers on page 94

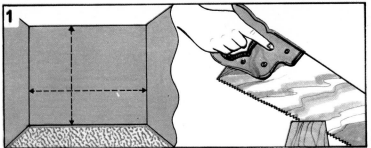

1 Measure height and width of wall. Cut battens to size. Using rawlplugs and drill, screw to wall.

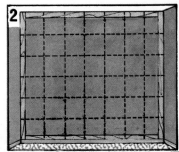

2 Mark off the size of Perspex panels on the wall. Remember to start at *outer* edges of battens.

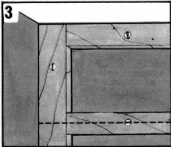

3 Measure horizontal lines between battens and cut across battens to size. Screw them to walls, along marked horizontal lines.

4 Prime and paint battens to match existing wall colour. Leave to dry.

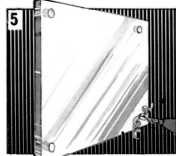

5 Drill holes at each corner of Perspex panels, 1.25cm in from edges.

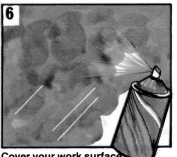

6 Cover your work surface carefully. Experiment first. Then, on one side of each panel spray on a mottled design in two toning shades.

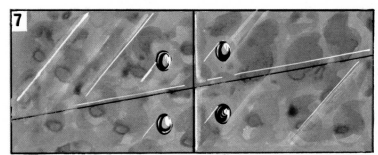

7 Cover surface of each panel thoroughly. When dry, *turning painted side to wall,* affix panels to battens with mirror screws. Ensure that all edges butt up closely.

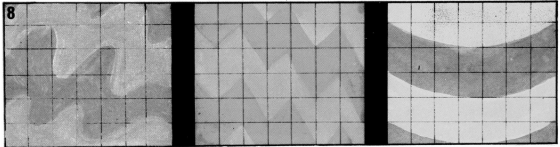

8 *Alternative designs:* It is best to keep to free and abstract effects, and not to use too many colours. Gold and silver are very effective on Perspex. Or you can achieve an attractive speckled effect, through which your wall colour will show, by spraying panels very lightly with a contrasting colour. Each square represents one Perspex panel.

Outdoors Indoors

Even on wintry days, it feels like summer in this garden room. Choose a dark, rich colour for the walls. For flowers and greenery all the year round, you can train decorative climbing plants up the white trellis—we suggest Russian ivy, climbing geraniums and jasmine for a start—and hang up your more delicate garden perennials in pots to keep them safe from frost in the winter. Paint some old wooden furniture white, cover the floor with grass-green carpeting (or sisal)—and enjoy your indoor garden all the year round. (Alternatively, just one wall covered as described opposite is attractive, particularly if the room is large.)

YOU WILL NEED:
Primer
Emulsion for walls
Gloss for trellis
Wooden trellis
Tenon saw
50 × 22mm wooden
  battens
Drill
Rawlplugs
Screwdriver · Screws
Hammer
Nails
Cup hooks
Countersink

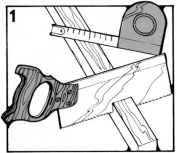

1 Measure along top and bottom (above skirting-board) of each wall. Cut battens to size for both measurements.

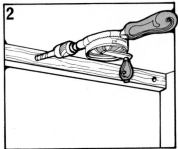

2 Starting with top battens, drill holes through wood and into wall at about 46cm intervals.

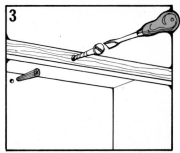

3 Using rawlplugs, screw top battens into place along each wall.

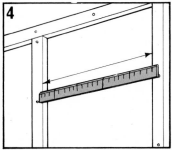

4 Repeat with bottom battens, screwing them into wall just above skirting board.

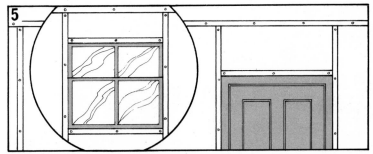

5 Measure distance from top to the bottom batten on each wall. You will need upright battens at about 1m intervals along each wall and up sides of doors and windows. Cut upright battens to size. Drill and screw into place.

6 Paint walls and battens with emulsion paint, having primed battens first

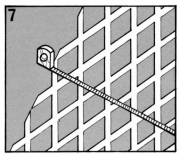

7 Measure surface area to be covered by trellis. Remember trellis must be *fully extended*.

8 Paint trellis first with primer, then with gloss paint, on *both* sides. Leave to dry.

9 Attach trellis to battens with small nails. Take care to match joins.

10 Touch up nail heads with gloss paint. Arrange tubs of climbing plants along walls and tie in the stalks to the trellis to start training them. Hang pots from cup hooks higher up.

Child's Play

Easy-to-clean floors are a must in a child's room—but they needn't be dull. In this playroom, the floor has been painted with the new, tough polyurethane paints which dry to a washable crack-proof finish. Opposite we give you some more suggestions for painted floor designs and overleaf we show you how to paint the giant checker board.

N.B. This treatment is not recommended for rooms with underfloor heating or very uneven floor surfaces. The 'growing tree' on the wall is fun for all the children—as they grow, hang apples, each marked with a child's name, to show the new height See page 47 for how to make it.

YOU WILL NEED:
Hardboard to cover entire
 floor area
Tenon saw
Hammer
Coppered hardboard pins
Plastic wood and/or filler
Coarse sandpaper
Primer · Undercoat
Orange, black and white
 polyurethane gloss paint
Rigid rule
5cm set-square
5cm-wide masking tape
Cutting-in tool
Paint brushes

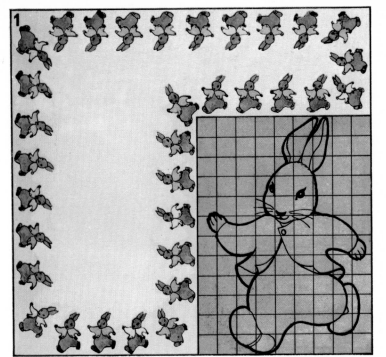

Run, Rabbit, Run. This idea is especially suitable for irregular-shaped rooms. You can make the rabbits big or small by altering the scale. Our scale is one square to 2.5cm.

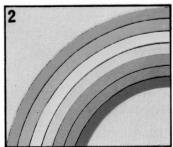

Over the Rainbow. A gay and colourful design for a little girl's room.

Hello, Sunshine! Brighten up your baby's room with this simple sunburst.

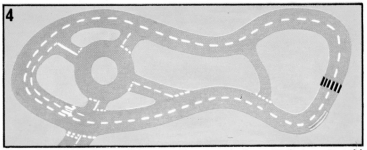

Model Road. Little boys will have endless fun playing with their cars on this busy roadway.

These slanting stripes are an effective way of treating the floor in a long, narrow room.

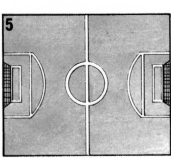

Indoor Games. Children can play all sorts of games on the painted football pitch.

Highway Code. They're never too young to learn the right way.

45

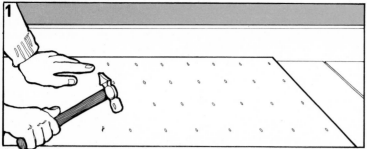

1 Measure floor area. Saw hardboard panels to size. Ensure that floor is even and remove all protruding nails, etc. Starting at corner, lay first panel *smooth side up.* Using coppered hardboard pins, nail to floor in 15cm grid.

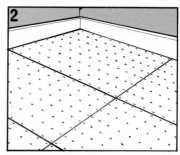

2 Repeat until floor is covered, ensuring panels fit closely.

3 Fill any small holes or gaps with plastic wood or filler. Sand when dry. Prime and undercoat hardboard. Leave to dry.

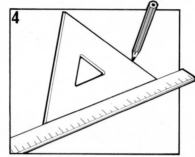

4 Using set-square and rule, draw a square 91 × 91cm on floor in selected position, well clear of door.

5 Stick masking tape along outside edge of square. Paint within this area with two coats white polyurethane. Leave to dry.

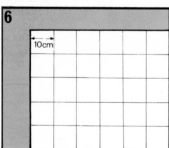

6 Mark off 10cm sections along all edges. Using rule, join marks with pencil, forming a board of 64 squares in all.

7 Using a cutting-in tool for straight edges, paint alternate squares with black polyurethane. Leave to dry. Remove tape.

8 Masking inner edge of board with tape to protect black and white edges, paint remainder of floor area with two coats orange polyurethane. Work outwards from checker board. Leave to dry.

Growing Tree

YOU WILL NEED:
Brown wrapping paper
Coloured paper in shades of
  red and green
Wallpaper paste
Paste brush
Scissors
Clear polyurethane gloss
  varnish
Brown poster paint
Pencil · Squared-up pattern
  paper
Paint brush

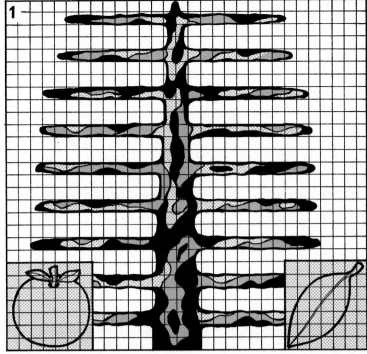

1

Use this picture as a guide for your design. For the tree, one of our squares equals 6cm. For the apple and leaves, one square equals 1.5cm.

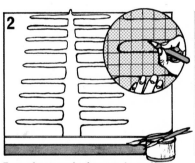

2 Transfer the design on to pattern paper. Trace the outline of a tree on the wall in brown paint.

3 Cover the area within the design with wallpaper paste to act as a size coat.

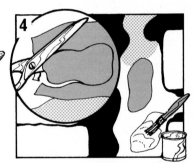

4 Cut out and paste pieces of brown wrapping paper in varying shades on to the trunk and branch areas of the tree.

5 Cut out and arrange green paper into clusters of leaves as shown in our picture.

6 Cut out an apple for each child. Put the child's name and the date on it. Paste to tree at appropriate height.

ANNE
5·4·75

7 Varnish your collage carefully with clear polyurethane gloss varnish.

Crowning Glory

Use the wall behind your bed as the central decorative feature of your room. In this bedroom a lavish swathe of material has been suspended from a brass crown, draped over two attractive brass tie-backs and allowed to fall to the floor. The amount of material and lining (either matching or contrasting) you need will depend on the height of your room. Calculate for two lined 'curtains', each 1 metre wide and twice the length of your floor-to-ceiling measurement.

YOU WILL NEED:
Heavy-weight curtain material
Lining
Matching sewing thread
Decorative fringe to edge
    side and bottom of curtains
Brass crown, plus own
    screws*
2 brass curtain tie-backs,
    screws
8 large curtain hooks
Drill · Rawlplugs
Screwdriver · Screws
1.25cm-wide tape

*From large department
    stores

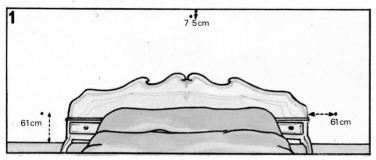

Mark position for crown, 7.5cm below ceiling and centred over the bed. Mark position for tie-backs, 61cm from each edge of bed and 61cm up from floor.

Using drill and rawl-plugs (see page 43). screw crown and tie-backs to marked positions.

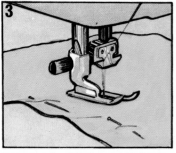

Cut curtain fabric and lining to measure. Pin right sides together, leaving bottom seam open. Machine, turn and press.

Turn in 2.5cm along bottom edges of curtain and lining. Machine these together, edge to edge. Press.

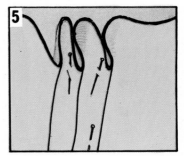

To form pleats for curtain heading, fold and pin curtain into triple folds each 2.5cm deep.

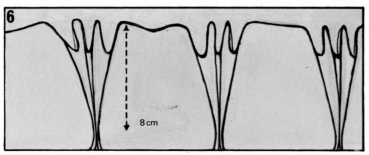

Form first group of pleats 2.5cm along from outer edge of each curtain. Starting 8cm down from top edge, sew pleats together to a depth of 1.5cm.

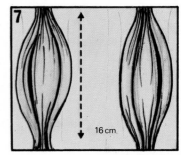

Measure 16cm below this and again sew pleats together to a depth of 1.5cm.

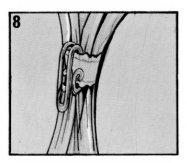

Sew on tapes to secure pleats at back. Slide hooks into tapes.

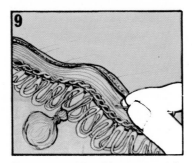

Pin and machine fringe to curtain edge at one side and along the bottom.

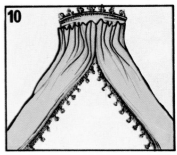

Hook curtains through holes in the crown and adjust them over the tie-backs so that they hang gracefully.

49

Headline News

Attractive bedheads are not only expensive to buy: it is often difficult to find one to match your existing décor. Our alternative is to hang soft cushions, covered to match your bedspread, against the wall. You can order a pole that measures the full width of your bed from your d-i-y shop or local ironmonger. Matching brass end-fittings come in a variety of decorative shapes and sizes. When estimating how much material you need, remember to make allowance for a 1.5cm seam.
N.B. For single beds, only one cushion is necessary.

YOU WILL NEED:
1 brass pole 4.5cm in
   diameter
2 decorative end-fittings
2 wall-fixing brackets to
   support pole
Rawlplugs · Drill
Screwdriver · Screws
2 foam-rubber pads, each
   half width of
   bed × 43cm × 5cm
2 zips, 20cm long
Material to cover pads plus
   33cm
Matching sewing
   thread · Pins

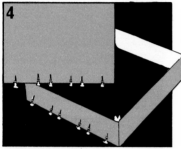

1

For covers: cut out two pieces of material same size as pad top plus 1.5cm all round; four strips 8cm wide to cover sides of pads.

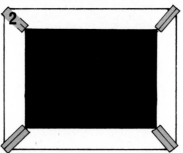

2

Machine the four strips into a rectangle, mitring corners. Trim seams. Press.

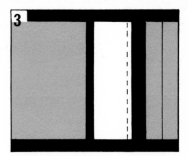

3

For loops: cut three strips 11.5cm wide × 16.5cm long. Fold each lengthways; machine along open sides. Trim seams, turn. Press.

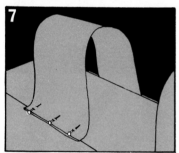

4

Mark with pins three openings, 5cm wide, for loops on one edge of fabric top, and at outer edge of rectangle, to match.

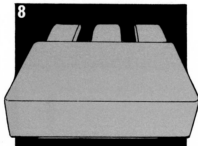

5

With right side facing, pin one end of loops on to fabric top as shown.

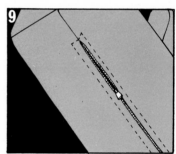

6

Right sides facing, machine rectangle around top. Trim seams. Press.

7

Pin free ends of loops into rectangle openings, right side facing, matching seam allowances.

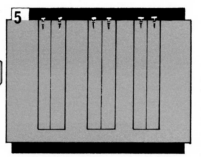

8

Right sides facing, machine cushion sections together, leaving 20cm open along bottom seam for zip. Trim seams, turn and press.

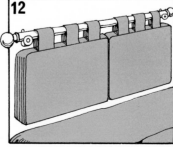

9

Pin, tack and stitch zip into open bottom seam.

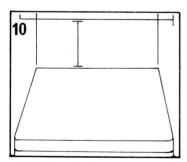

10

For wall brackets: mark 5cm from each side and 61cm from top of mattress.

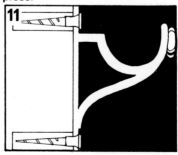

11

Using rawlplugs and drill, screw brackets into wall at marked positions.

12

Put pads into covers. Slide loops over pole. Affix pole to brackets. Screw on decorative ends.

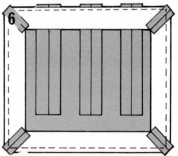

Fabric Fashion

Fabric on the wall is one of the prettiest ideas for bedroom décor. Our picture, above, shows walls covered in a large-patterned, heavy cotton fabric; our instructions opposite and over the page show a lighter, check cotton material which would look charming in a little girl's bedroom. Because the pattern-matching is so easy, far less of this check material would be needed. The effect is cosy and relaxing—and for a total look you can match up your curtains and covers. Whichever look you decide to go for, we recommend furnishing fabric, because of its greater width and hard-wearing qualities. Measure your wall area (excluding doors, unless they are flush, and windows). The material must cover this area plus an extra metre. You will need enough braid to go round the top and bottom of each wall, down each corner and all round windows and door frames. For flush doors, buy extra material to door size and braid to go round the edges.

N.B. If you are planning to put a light-coloured material over a darker wall-surface, give the wall a coat of white emulsion first.

YOU WILL NEED:
Fabric
Matching sewing thread
2.5cm braid
Scissors
Non-metal spatula
Staple gun · Staples
Rubber-based adhesive
Screwdriver

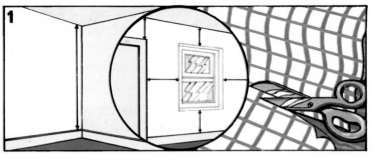

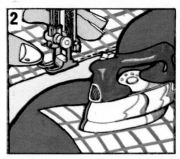

Check staples will go into walls and hold chosen fabric. Measure height of walls. Measure to edge of door and window frames. Cut fabric to size allowing 1.5cm extra on each length and 1.5cm extra round door and window openings.

Machine fabric into separate wall-size sheets. Press seams open.

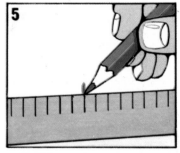

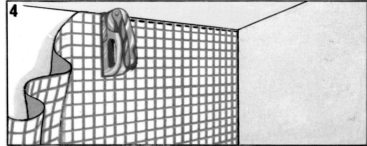

Check that sheets fit walls and that openings are correctly positioned. (You will need help with this).

Starting at upper right corner of first wall and keeping material taut, staple it into wall in a straight line as close as possible to the ceiling at 7cm intervals. Allow enough material to get a good grip on it when stretching it into corners.

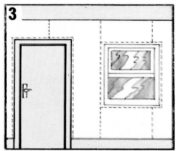

On skirting, measure off and mark centre bottom of wall. Position fabric down wall smoothly.

Smoothing and stretching fabric as you go, staple as close to skirting board as possible, working from centre to each side.

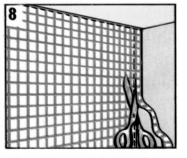

Starting at top and continuing to stretch fabric, staple down corners as close up to wall-angle as possible.

Trim off excess fabric. Repeat stapling along next wall. Fabric may overlap slightly owing to stretching.

At doors and windows, check fabric hangs smoothly. Keeping material taut, start stapling at corners.

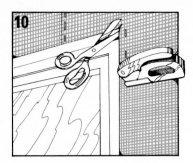

Before stapling along top, bottom and each side, ease fabric by snipping in 1.5cm at corners.

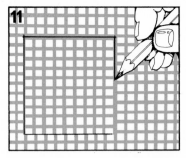

When walls are completed, locate and mark position of light switches under fabric.

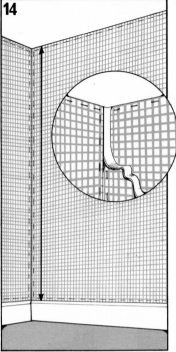

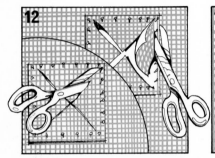

With pins, mark a square 5mm smaller than switch. Cut X in centre to within 1cm of corners. Trim off points.

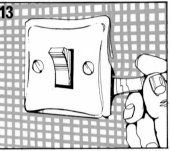

Loosen switch fitting. Using spatula *(N.B. not metal)*, tuck fabric behind fitting. Tighten screws.

Measure corners, ceiling to skirting board. Cut braid to size. Glue braid down corners to conceal staples and joins.

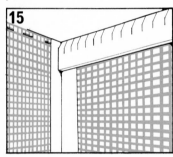

Measure all round ceiling. Cut and glue braid as above.

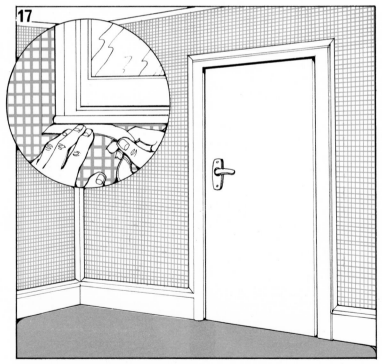

Repeat round skirting board.

Cut braid to size for trimming round windows and door frames. Mitre braid at all corners to fit smoothly.

18

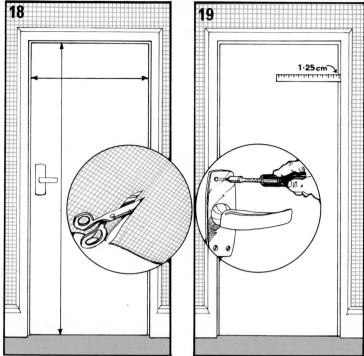

For flush doors, measure height and width. Cut material to size 1.25cm shorter and narrower.

19

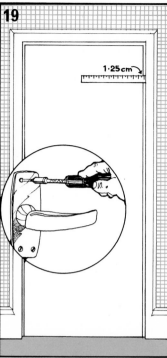

Remove door handle. Mark line 1.25cm away from door edges.

20

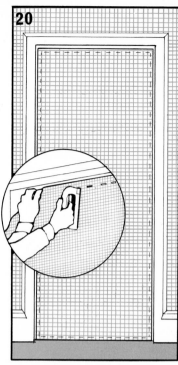

Staple fabric along line at top, bottom and sides. Keep fabric taut while stapling.

21

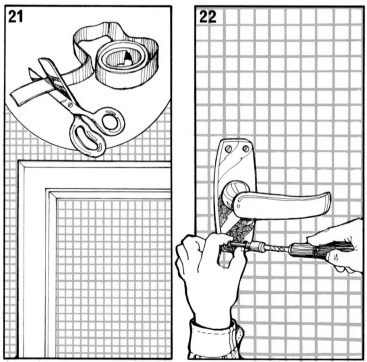

Measure round fabric edge. Cut braid to size. Glue over staples, mitring corners.

22

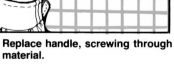

Replace handle, screwing through material.

23

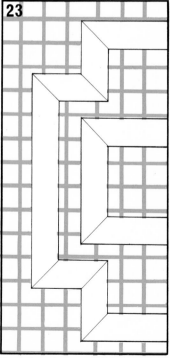

To make a feature of the braid, glue it in a pattern on fabric. Buy extra braid for this.

Deft Disguises

This bathroom window features an elegant screen (decorators call it a lambrequin) that adds colour but is also a practical way of hiding the gap between the edge of a roller or Roman blind and the window frame where you have a recessed window. For the lambrequin you need a sheet of hardboard 3.75cm wider and 7.5cm higher than the outside edge of the window frame and a length of fabric 7.5cm wider and longer than your hardboard. You will need enough battening to go up the sides and across the top of the frame of your hardboard cut-out. See page 58 for materials and instructions for making the bath screen.

YOU WILL NEED:
Battens, 20 × 75mm
Coppered hardboard pins
No. 10 woodscrews
Hammer
Screwdriver
Fabric (as above)
Rubber-based adhesive
Scissors
Felt-tip pen
Padsaw

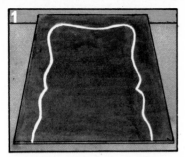

Using felt-tip pen, draw design, as above, on hardboard. At its narrowest, the design must be wider than window frame itself.

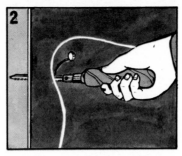

Next, cut out the design round the outline with padsaw.

Measure sides and top of outside edge of window frame. Cut three battens to these sizes.   N.B. Top batten will be width of window plus thickness of two side battens.

Screw battens to outside edge of frame at sides and top, as shown.

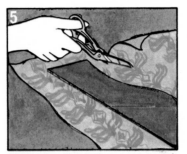

Place hardboard on material. Leaving a 7.5cm overlap at sides and top, cut cloth with 5cm overlap in centre.

Using pins, nail hardboard, smooth side out, to battens at 5cm intervals.

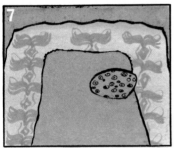

Cover hardboard with glue. Apply material, smoothing down with sponge. Remember to leave overlaps.

Apply glue to side edges of hardboard and battens.

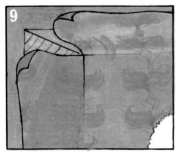

Trim and turn in overlaps at corners and stick down material so that it covers hardboard edges and battens.

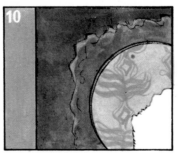

At inner edge, apply glue, to a depth of 5cm, all round back of hardboard.

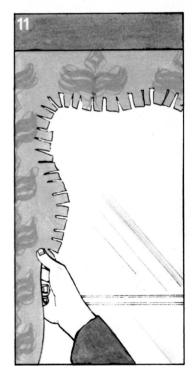

Snip overlap at 1.25cm intervals; turn in and press firmly into place.

Bath Screen

As you can see from the picture, you will be constructing a frame from floor to ceiling at the end of your bath. Measure the height of your room and the width of the bath. Buy enough battening for twice the height and three times the width; enough 6mm hardboard to box in the end of the bath; a sheet of Panelaire the width of the bath and the height from the top of the bath to the ceiling; and enough moulding for twice the height of your room and twice the width of the bath.

YOU WILL NEED:

Wooden battens, 25 × 25mm
Hardboard, 6mm thick
Panelaire*
Pin hammer
Screwdriver · Screws
Coppered hardboard pins
Rebated half-round wooden
    moulding
Panel pins
Mitre box · Tenon saw
Primer · Undercoat · Gloss
    paint
Wood glue
Brush
Rawlplugs · Drill

*See list of suppliers on
    page 94

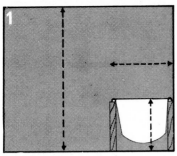

1 Saw five battens to size: two to height of room, three to width of bath less the thickness of the two uprights.

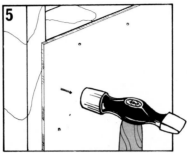

2 With middle cross-batten placed at height of bath, glue and screw battens together to form frame.

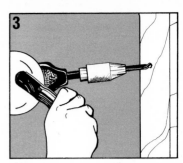

3 Using rawlplugs and drill (see page 43), screw frame to wall, ceiling and floor.

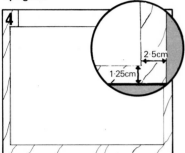

4 Saw hardboard 2.5cm narrower and 1.25cm shorter than the outside measure of the lower section of frame.

2·5cm
1·25cm

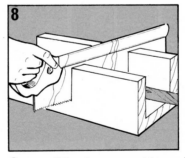

5 Using coppered pins, nail hardboard to bottom section of frame, smooth side out.

6 Saw Panelaire to size, 2.5cm narrower and 1.25cm shorter than the outside measure of the upper section of frame.

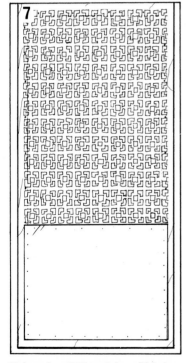

7 Using pins, fit Panelaire within top section of frame as shown, so that it is flush to hardboard edge.

8 Saw moulding to surround frame, using mitre box for 45° corners.

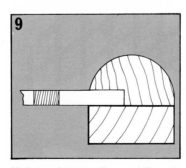

9 Using pins, nail moulding to frame. The rebate will fit over Panelaire edge to give a neat finish.

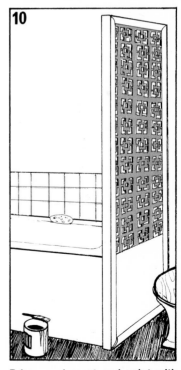

10 Prime, undercoat and paint with one coat of gloss. Take care not to overload brush when painting Panelaire.

Bring Down the Ceiling

When it comes to decorating, bathrooms are often neglected, yet they are in fact ideal places for letting yourself go with adventurous ideas. Here we show you how to cope with a small, high-ceilinged bathroom. It is made cosy and glamorous with a sloping ceiling canopy and brown velvety felt on the walls. To estimate the material needed for the canopy, measure the width of the room, add on 5cm; measure the length of the room, add on a third of this length. You need enough material to cover this area. If your material is patterned, remember to allow for pattern-matching. There is an alternative design for a canopy on page 63. For the felt: measure your wall area, excluding doors and windows; you will need felt to cover the walls, plus 10cm extra on each length to allow for shrinkage.

YOU WILL NEED:
For the walls:
Felt (see left)
Heavy-duty wallpaper paste
Stainless wallpaper paste
Rigid rule · Stanley knife

For the canopy:
Material (see left)
Matching sewing thread
4 2cm brass case rods,
    2.5cm shorter than room
    width
8 end-fix sockets (with
    screws) for rods
Rawlplugs · Drill
Dressmaker's pins
Saucer, 15cm in diameter
Ruler · Pencil
Tape, 2.5cm wide, 4 times
    width of room, plus 20cm

Size entire wall area with heavy-duty wallpaper paste to provide strong base for felt. Allow to dry.

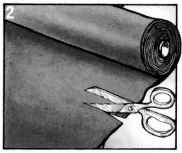

Cut felt into lengths which are 10cm longer than height of walls.

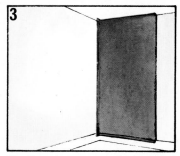

Starting at corner, apply stainless wallpaper paste *to wall*. Apply felt to wall. Allow 5cm overlap at top, bottom and corner side of felt.

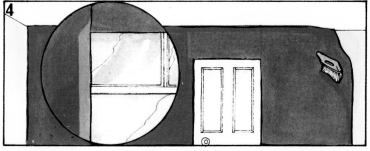

Paste next wall area and apply next strip of felt, allowing another 5cm overlap on side of felt already hung. Repeat until all walls are covered. N.B. Allow a 5cm overlap around door and window frames as well.

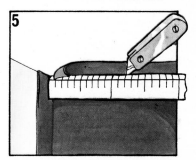

Leave felt to dry for 24 hours at minimum to allow for overall shrinkage. Trim overlaps, first at top, then bottom.

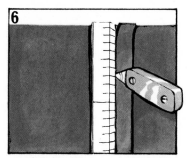

At centre joins, cut through the two pieces of overlapping felt with knife and remove excess so that edges butt-up closely.

Machine material into one large sheet, 10cm wider than room width, and the length of the room plus an extra third. Press seams open.

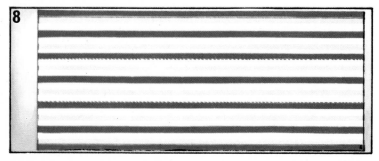

Machine 5cm hem along each side of sheet. Press. Lay sheet flat, right side up.

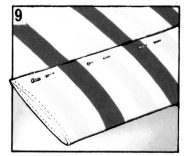

Fold back 15cm at either end (right sides inside). Pin along edges.

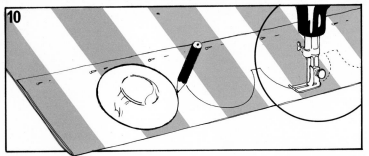

Using saucer and leaving 5cm between each scallop, draw scallop design along folded edges, placing saucer at centre of fold as shown above. Machine along pencilled scallop lines.

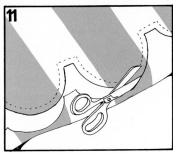

Cut away surplus material, 1.25cm away from stitching.

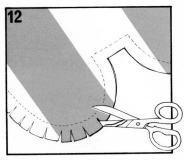

To ease, make snips with scissors round edge of scallops at 1.25cm intervals, taking care not to cut into machine stitching.

Remove pins. Turn scallops right side out. Press.

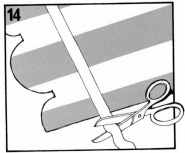

Lay sheet flat, wrong side up. Cut tape into four pieces, each 5cm longer than sheet width. Turn, and sew down 2.5cm of tape ends.

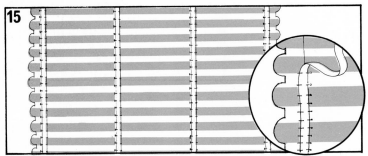

Pin tape along inner edges of scallop borders, and also at two equal intervals across width of material.

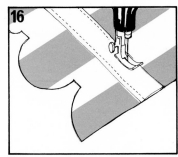

Leaving ends open for inserting rods, machine both sides of tapes down on to sheet, 3mm from tape edges.

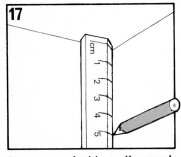

At corner of side walls, mark points for rod sockets 5cm below ceiling. At opposite corners, mark points 30cm below ceiling.

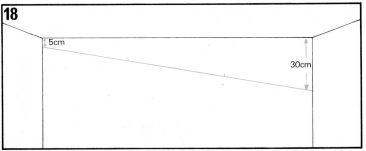

Draw sloping line joining the two marks. Along this line mark off two more socket fixtures at equal intervals.

19

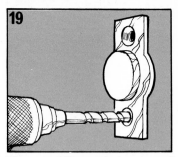

Place end-fix sockets at each marked position. Drill holes in walls through screw holes.

20

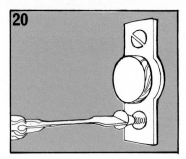

Plug holes in walls. Screw fixtures into place.

21

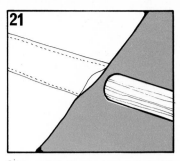

Slide rods between tapes and mat ‑ erial.

22

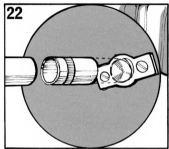

Place rod ends into sockets.

23

You will find it necessary to smooth canopy along rods, distributing it as evenly as possible.

24

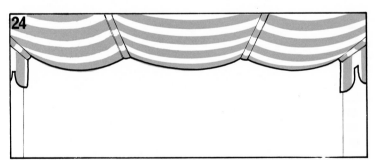

If you decide to have a flat, rather than a sloping canopy, it is easy to achieve: merely follow steps 7 to 16. Then, at corner of side walls, mark points for sockets, both 30cm below ceiling.

25

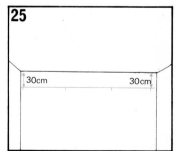

Draw a straight line, joining the marks. Mark for two more sockets between these points and then continue from 19 to 23.

26

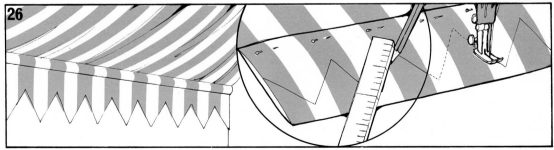

For a straight-edged canopy, follow steps 7 to 9. Then, with a ruler, draw zigzag design 8cm deep along edges.

Machine along the zigzag line. Then continue exactly as above, from step 11.

Bathing Beauty

This bath has been boxed in with cupboards and a decorated bath panel. In the following instructions for making these, the quantity of materials given has been based on a standard bath, 170cm long and 53cm high. Adjust the measurements to fit your own bath. Sheets of mirror-mosaic tiling can be bought from many d-i-y shops and are easy to apply to a smooth wall surface: however, you *must* use a water-resistant adhesive.

YOU WILL NEED:
12mm chipboard sheet,
  53 × 170cm
6.5m battening, 50 × 50mm
Wood glue · Saw
Mitre box · Plastic wood
Primer · Undercoat
Brown and blue gloss paint
Brushes · Pencil · Rule
Screws · Screwdriver
Sandpaper · Panel pins
Nails · Nail punch
6m of 25mm decorative
  wooden moulding

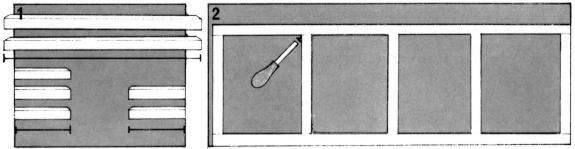

Saw two pieces of batten into 170cm lengths and five into 47cm lengths. These will form frame for chipboard.

Glue and nail battens together to form frame. The three centre battens should be placed at intervals of 55cm.

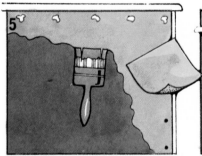

Fit frame to side of bath by wedging it under the bath rim. Screw base batten to floor.

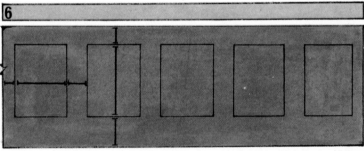

Nail chipboard to frame along top, bottom, side and centre battens.

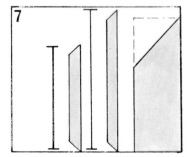

Punch nails below the surface and stop up holes with plastic wood. Sand when dry. Prime, undercoat and paint with one coat of gloss.

Mark five rectangles on panel, each 33cm high and 24cm wide, to lie 10cm from top of the panel. Mark first rectangle 5cm in from side edge of panel, leaving 10cm between designs.

Using mitre box to form 45° angles at both ends, saw ten pieces of moulding 24cm long and ten 33cm long.

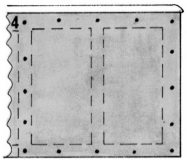

Prime, undercoat and paint mouldings with contrasting gloss. When dry, glue and nail to marked rectangles with panel pins. If necessary, touch up pin heads with matching gloss.

Top Light

A soft, all-over light is particularly attractive in bathrooms, kitchens and halls. Here we show you a bathroom with a false ceiling of Perspex panels through which the fluorescent lighting is agreeably diffused. To work out how many panels you will need, find the total square measurement of your ceiling, then divide it into equal squares. Our instructions are for a room 183 × 244cm and the panels are each 61cm square. (Adjust the quantities and panel size to your own requirements.) This treatment is not recommended for irregularly-shaped rooms.

YOU WILL NEED:
2.54m L-shaped lath, 38mm
**   thick**
3m T-shaped lath, 75mm
**   thick**
12 Perspex panels,
**   61cm-square**
Rawlplugs · Drill
Screwdriver · Screws
Wood glue
Primer · Undercoat · Gloss
**   paint**
Paint brush
Mitre box · Saw
Rigid rule · Pencil

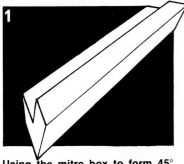

1 Using the mitre box to form 45° angles each end, saw L-lath into fourteen 61cm sections.

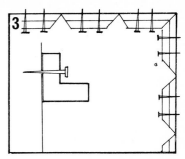

2 Mark continuous line around walls, 30cm below ceiling. Mark off line every 61cm.

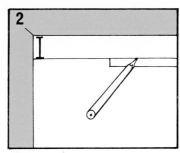

3 Starting at corner, using drill and rawlplugs, screw laths to marked positions on line. Screw *flat side* downwards.

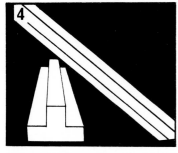

4 Using mitre box to form double 45° angles each end, saw T-lath into 61cm sections.

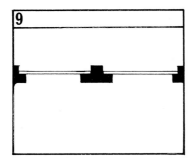

5 Glue and screw together two laths, as shown. To form first frame, glue and screw these laths into corner-wall laths. (Ask someone to support frame until you've assembled more.)

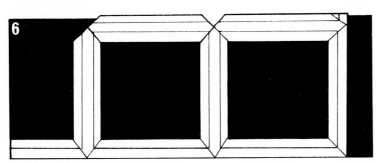

6 Assemble next frame as first. Glue and screw into adjoining wall section.

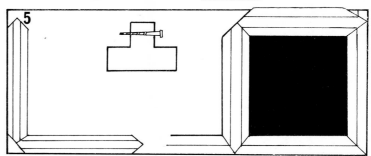

7

11	10	7	6
12	8	4	3
9	5	2	1

Continue to assemble and install frames in sequence shown.

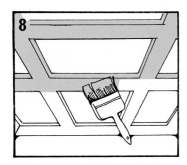

8 When framework is completed, prime, undercoat and paint with one coat of gloss.

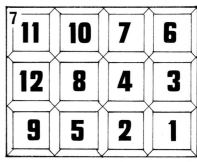

9 Lift Perspex panels and slide through sideways. Lower gently into position on laths.

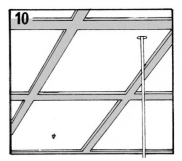

10 If you have a light cord, drill hole in appropriate Perspex panel before installing. Thread cord through hole.

On the Tiles

Ceramic tiles are the most satisfactory surface around a bath, especially if there is a shower attachment. In this glamorous bathroom, old decorated tiles have been mixed with modern white ones to form a striking pattern. If you hunt through antique shops you can still find old tiles but carefully chosen modern ones can be equally attractive. Here we show you how to reproduce the above pattern on your bath panel. The quantity of tiles, shown below, are for a standard bath, 170cm long and 53cm high. On pages 70 and 71, we also show you how to make two sorts of splashproof shower barrier: plastic and cotton curtains, as in the photograph, and a folding Perspex screen. The measurements are for a standard bath and for a room 244cm high. Remember to adjust the materials and measurements to your own requirements and always allow a little extra for spoilage or mistakes!

YOU WILL NEED:
Ceramic wall tiles,
  100 × 100mm:
  97 white, 15 for vertical
  pattern, 31 for horizontal
  pattern
Water-resistant tile adhesive
Plastic spreader
Spirit level
Water-resistant grout
2 battens 170cm long,
  25 × 15mm
Synthetic sponge
Soft cloth
Hammer · Nails
Short stick with rounded end

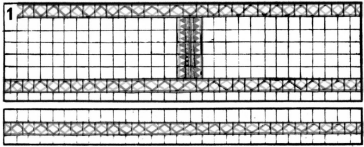

Top: wall panel. *Bottom:* bath panel. Each square represents one tile. Follow these diagrams to reproduce wall patterns and bath panel. For a longer area, centre vertical pattern and add on tiles each end.

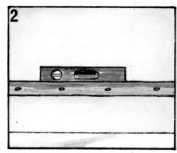

Using spirit level for horizontal, lightly nail batten to wall, with top edge of batten 10cm above top of bath.

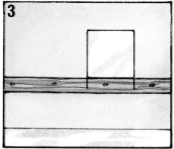

Mark centre of batten. Place centre tile over mark and pencil off width. Mark off widths of remaining tiles along batten.

Cover the wall with tile adhesive for first row of tiles. Starting at one end and following marked widths affix first row above batten.

Continue tiling, working in rows and ensuring that spacer lugs of adjoining tiles touch. When top four rows are completed, remove batten.

If bath edge is not straight, tiles along bottom row may need some trimming. (See page 23 for how to cut ceramic tiles.)

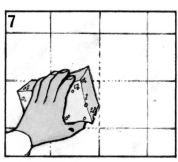

Complete last row of tiling. Using sponge, grout tiled area. Wipe off excess grout with damp cloth when nearly dry.

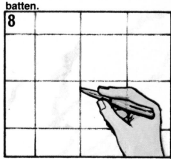

Using stick with rounded end, rub along grouted joins gently to ensure a smooth, neat finish.

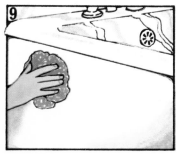

Before tiling bath panel, ensure that it is strong, clean and unwarped.

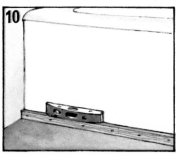

Using spirit level, nail batten to base of panel, to act as guide line and remain as skirting board.

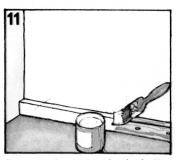

Prime, undercoat and paint batten with one coat of gloss. Tile panel as in step 1 above. Wait three days before using bath, to allow grout to dry really thoroughly.

Shower Curtains

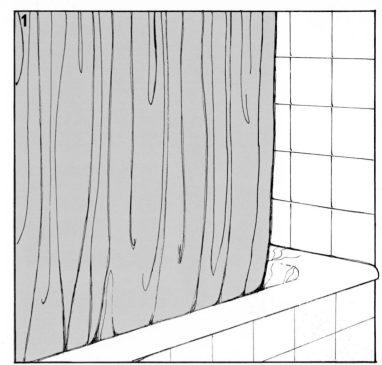

In this close-up of the shower curtain, you can see how the plastic lining curtain should hang *inside* the bath when drawn, giving complete protection from splashes.

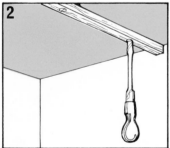

Using rawlplugs and drill, screw batten to ceiling, parallel to edge of bath.

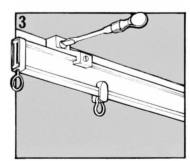

Prime and paint batten to match ceiling. Screw rail to batten edge facing the room, not the bath.

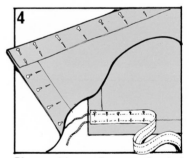

Pin, machine and press a hem at bottom and sides of fabric curtain. Turn in 4cm at top. Pin tape on raw edge, 2cm below heading.

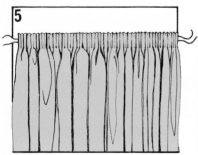

Using strings on tape, gather curtain to a width of 170cm.

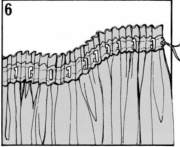

Insert curtain hooks into tape and into prepared holes on plastic curtain.

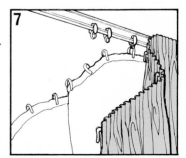

Making sure that shower curtain is on the bath side, hang curtains on alternate hooks, starting with the fabric curtain.

Shower Screen

YOU WILL NEED:
5m single channel wood
moulding, 35 × 15mm
Wire nails · Rawlplugs
Hammer · Hand drill
Wood glue · Screwdriver
3 5cm flat chrome cabinet
hinges
Thin sheet cloudy Perspex,
76cm wide × 170cm high
Primer · Undercoat · Gloss
paint
Paint brushes

This decorative shower screen is hinged to the wall at the edge of the bath so that it can be folded back when not in use.

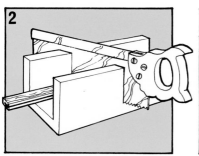

For frame, saw four pieces of moulding, two to 170cm and two to 78cm in length. Make 45° angles at both ends in mitre box.

Prime and paint moulding strips with one coat of gloss. Check that Perspex fits by placing moulding loosely round it.

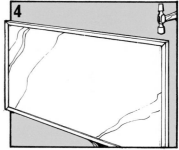

With Perspex in place, glue and nail frame together at corners. Touch up nail heads with gloss if necessary.

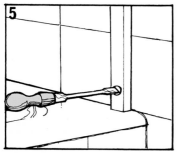

Using rawlplugs and a hand drill, screw batten between bath top and ceiling. Prime and paint to match wall.

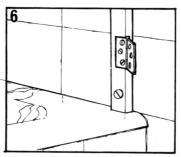

Mark batten for position of hinges 5cm from top and bottom and at centre point in between. Screw hinges on to batten.

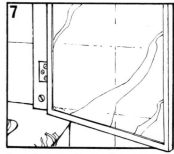

Leaving a 2cm clearance at bottom, offer up frame to batten and screw hinges into frame.

Try a Tent

In a compact modern house, a new baby can cause a space panic! Many older houses, however, have small rooms which are often used merely as junk areas. Here is an idea to turn a small room into a really pretty nest for the new arrival—particularly if the room has an unattractively high ceiling: make the room into a 'tent' and it will become one of the most charming features in your home. Measure the length and width of the room. Buy enough material to cover the width and twice the length. Your battening has to go all round the walls, and you need enough decorative fringe to go *twice* round the walls. A light-weight fabric is recommended for this project, to hang in soft folds.

YOU WILL NEED:
Material (see left)
Decorative fringe
25 × 50mm wooden battens
Saw · Hammer
Screwdriver · Screws
Rawlplugs · Drill
Rigid rule · Pencil
Staple gun · Staples
Scissors
Thick string
Drawing pins
4 bamboo poles to height of
**   room**
Masonry nails
5cm brass hook

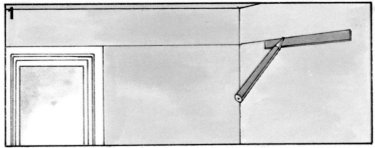

1 With pencil and rule, draw a continuous line all round walls, either at the level of the door top, or at the top of window frame, whichever is the higher.

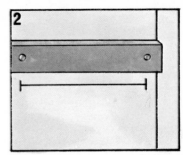

2 Starting at a corner, screw battens on this line at 55cm intervals, using drill and rawlplugs.

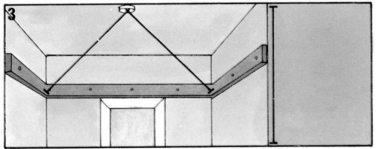

3 Measure from centre of ceiling to battens at corner. Cut material into four lengths corresponding to this measurement; reserve enough material for a border 18cm deep to go all around room.

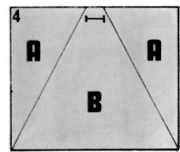

4 Cut lengths into triangles as shown, the flat apex of triangle B to measure 5cm across.

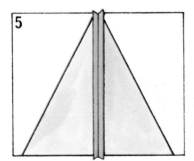

5 Machine pieces marked A together at longest edge. Press.

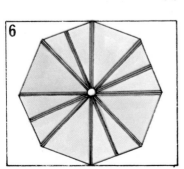

6 Machine all triangles together to form a circle with a hole in the middle as shown.

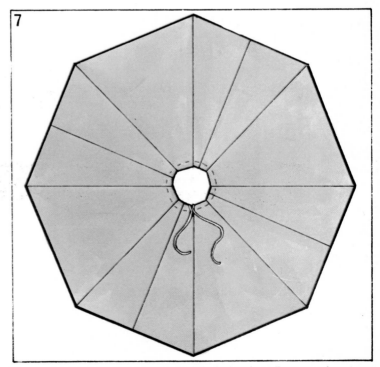

7 Turn and machine 1.5cm hem around circle, leaving a 7mm opening at one seam. Cut string double the circumference of circle and thread through hem.

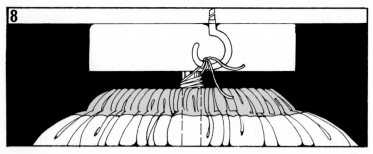

8 Remove centre light's shade. Drill and plug ceiling and screw in hook next to light fitting. Slip canopy over light fitting. Tie string tightly round top of light fixture and round hook.

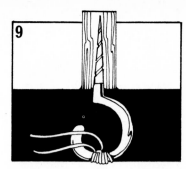

9 If no centre light fitting, simply drill and plug a hole at centre for hook. Screw in, and secure canopy to it.

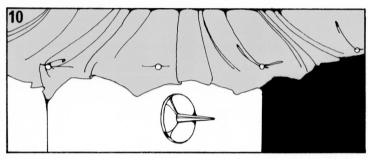

10 Using drawing pins, pin canopy edge to battens at corners and centre of each wall, ensuring that material is evenly distributed.

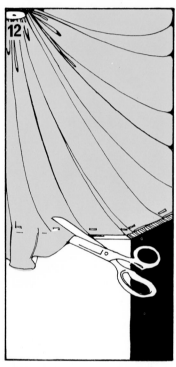

12 When stapling is completed, trim excess material along battens.

11 Starting at corner, staple edge of canopy to battens at 6.5cm intervals, pleating as you go to form folds. Do not worry if folds are irregular.

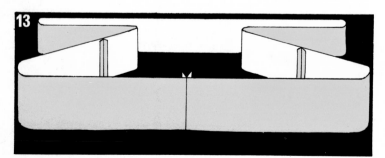

13 Cut remaining material into 18cm-wide strips to form border to go round room. Machine lengths together. Press.

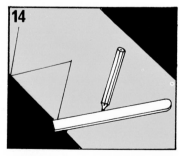

14 With pencil and rule, draw zigzag design round border, each zigzag measuring 7.5cm in depth.

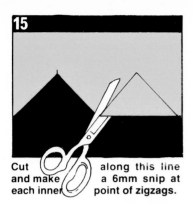

Cut along this line and make a 6mm snip at each inner point of zigzags.

Turn in and machine 1.25cm hem along straight edge of border. Press.

Right side of border facing, turn up and press a flat 6mm hem along zigzag edge.

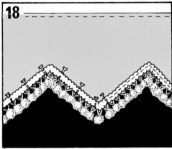

Pin and machine decorative fringe along 6mm turn-up of zigzag edge.

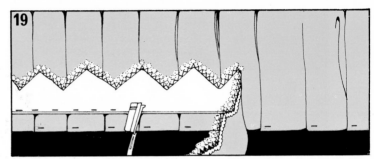

Holding border upside-down, staple it to battens along the 1.25cm hem, *above* stapling line for canopy.

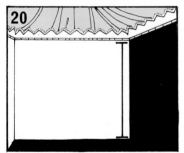

Keeping border turned up, measure from floor to battens at corners. Cut bamboo poles to this size.

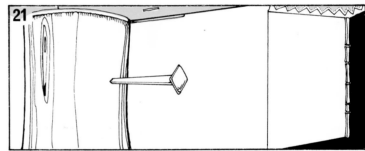

Place bamboo poles at room corners and nail to wall with masonry nails at top, bottom and centre.

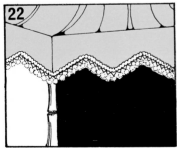

Fold border down over battens and tops of poles and smooth into place.

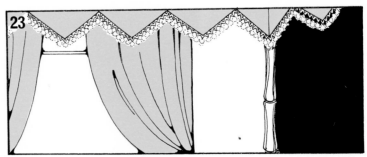

If you have enough material make matching curtains for window, for a cosy finishing touch!

Up the Garden Path

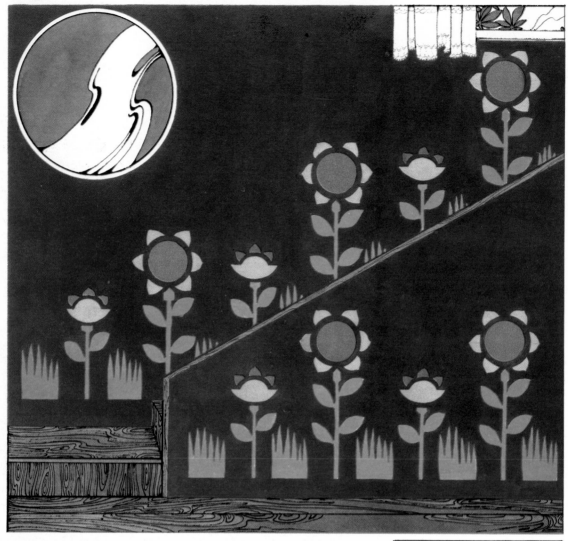

A narrow dark hall can be difficult to decorate successfully, yet your hall is a part of your home where you can experiment with bold ideas. Here we show how such a hall can become a 'garden path'. The walls and woodwork are painted throughout in a dark navy-blue gloss paint—gloss to reflect the available light. For instructions on painting walls and woodwork, see page 11. On the opposite page we show you how to make a frieze of stylized flowers which have been stencilled in gloss paint along the walls. Remember not to start any surface decoration until the paint on the walls and woodwork is thoroughly dry.

YOU WILL NEED:
Undercoat
Navy-blue gloss paint
Cardboard
Pencil
Squared-up pattern paper
Scissors
Small cans of orange, red
  and green gloss paint
Stipple brush
25mm paint brush

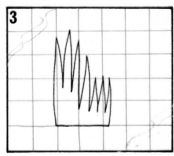

The 'grass' scales up to 30.5cm. In all these diagrams, one square equals 7.5cm.

Each square is 7.5 × 7.5cm. When scaled up, this flower will be 90cm high.

This flower scales up to 60cm in height. You can alter the scale if you want a smaller or a larger design.

Transfer designs from squared paper on to cardboard by pricking around the pattern edges with a sharp nail or pin.

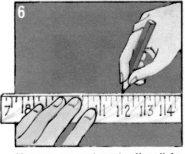

Shade in design area on the cardboard and cut out shaded area.

Measure up and mark off wall for each design. Leave a 30.5cm space between each design.

Apply stencil at marked position. Starting with largest flower, paint leaves with stipple brush. Apply other stencils, painting in all green areas.

When green areas are completed, paint in the red centre and the orange petals.

The stencil shapes may need two coats of paint to cover the navy-blue gloss effectively.

Dressing Up

Fitted cupboards all along one wall of a bedroom are practical and space saving—but they can look very dull. Here we show you how wallpaper and moulding can turn them into an extremely attractive wall-area that will match the rest of your room. (If your walls are painted, paint the cupboard doors to match and the mouldings, described opposite, in a contrasting colour.) You will need enough moulding to surround all the edges of the cupboard doors. Of course, you cannot apply moulding to sliding doors!

YOU WILL NEED:
Wallpaper to cover door
   surfaces
Decorative wooden
   moulding
Plastic wood
Panel pins
Pin hammer
Wood glue
Mitre box · Saw
Wallpaper paste · Brush
Paperhanger's brush
Sandpaper
Primer · Undercoat · Gloss
   paint
5cm paint brush
Screwdriver

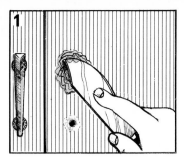

1. Remove cupboard handles. Stop up holes with plastic wood. Sand flush to surface when dry.

2. Cut wallpaper to size of doors matching pattern. Paste and apply, smoothing from centre outwards with paperhanger's brush.

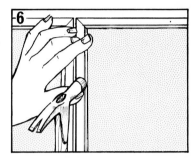

3. Measure along tops and bottoms of doors and down sides.

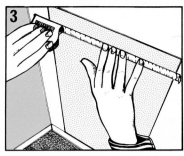

4. Cut moulding to size in four pieces (per door). Use mitre box to cut 45° angles at ends.

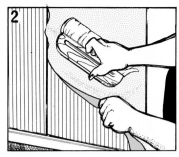

5. Paint mouldings with primer, undercoat and one coat of gloss. Leave to dry.

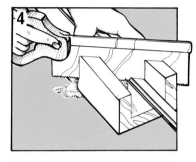

6. Glue mouldings flush to door edges. Nail every 25cm for extra strength.

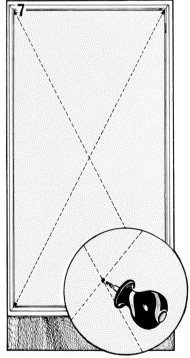

7. Measure and mark off for handles at centre of doors. Screw handles into position.

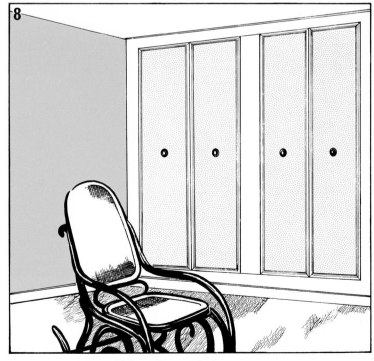

8. The finished doors, with handles attached.

Hide a Hole

If you have an awkward alcove, you can turn it into a space-saving cupboard with attractive folding doors. Here, instructions are given for covering the doors with fabric which matches the rest of the walls, but you can equally well cover them with matching wallpaper. To estimate the amount of material needed, measure each door, then add a 7.5cm overlap all round. Remember to allow for matching the pattern if you choose a patterned design. Folding-door gear, complete with instructions, can be purchased at any good d-i-y shop. Measure full width of alcove and buy gear to this measurement.

YOU WILL NEED:
Folding-door gear*
12mm blockboard for doors
Tenon saw
3 face-fixing cabinet hinges,
  with own screws
Screwdriver · Screws
Material to cover doors
1 handle with screws, per
  door
Wallpaper paste · Brush
Non-staining fabric glue
Retractable rule

*See list of suppliers on
  page 94

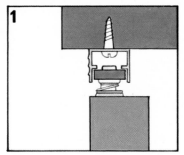

1 Install folding-door gear, following maker's instructions.

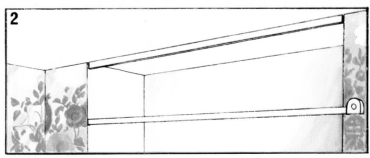

2 Measure blockboard for doors. *For width:* divide width of alcove into equal parts, then subtract 5mm per part. *For height:* measure from bottom of folding-door gear to floor, then subtract 10mm.

3 Cut blockboard to size.

4 Coat door front, edges, and to a depth of 6.25cm inside it with wallpaper paste. Allow to dry.

5 Cut fabric panels to same size as doors, plus 7.5cm overlap all round. Glue to door. Smooth over with soft cloth.

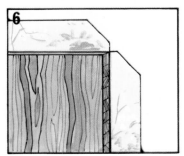

6 Allow to dry. Turn doors over and cut material, as shown, for mitred corners.

7 Apply glue to edges and back of door to a depth of 6.25cm.

8 Stick down overlap.

9 Screw 3 hinges to *inner* edge of doors, at centre, and at 15cm from top and bottom of doors.

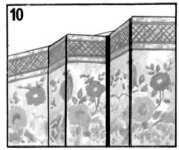

10 Hang doors on gear, following makers' instructions.

11 Affix handles.

Patio Playtime

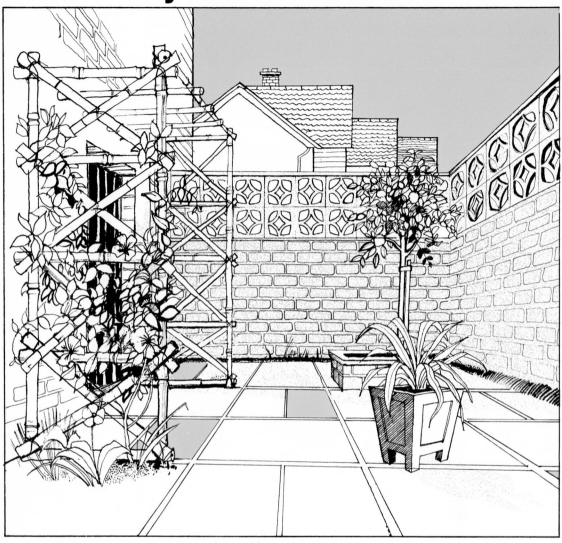

This small yard has been converted into an attractive patio by developing simple design features. The decorative concrete blocks give privacy and contrast with the rough, painted brick walls. The two-colour paving stones have been laid in a a formal pattern, highlighted by coloured mortar joins (see page 84). Buy enough stones to cover ground area, remembering that if you want to build the lean-to, to leave the earth uncovered for a flower bed 30cm wide × 137cm long. You will also need enough bedding sand to cover your entire ground area, excluding flower beds, to a depth of 2.5cm. The bamboo lean-to is an unusual and exotic feature. We give directions (see page 85) for a frame 243cm high, 370cm long and 122cm deep. You can adapt these measurements as required. When your climbing plants have grown over the bamboo poles, you will have a colourful, shady bower from which you can enjoy the view over your re-modelled patio!

YOU WILL NEED:
Enough concrete screen
   blocks for two courses the
   length of your walls
Block coping pieces to the
   same length
Cement, lime, sand mixed in
   proportion 1:1:6
Spirit level
Trowel
String
Pointed stick, 1cm wide

1

You will be working along each wall away from the corner of adjoining walls. Mix mortar to stated proportion. Place layer of mortar 2cm thick, and width and length of each block, at corner for first blocks. Press blocks into place.

2

Check with spirit level that blocks are straight. Measure off widths of blocks along each wall.

3

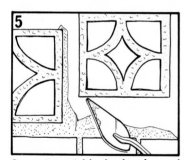

Following instructions for mortar in box 1, cement end-blocks in place at last full-measured width.

4

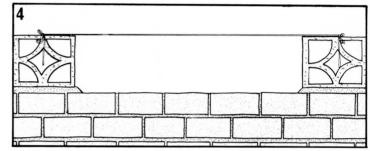

Stretch string tautl between end-blocks to provide a straight guide line. On old, uneven walls, you must compensate for irregularities by laying a thicker layer of mortar under the first course of blocks as necessary.

5

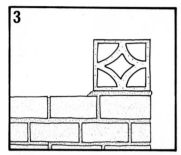

Cement next blocks in place at corners, spreading mortar on wall and in a layer 1.5cm thick up side of block.

6

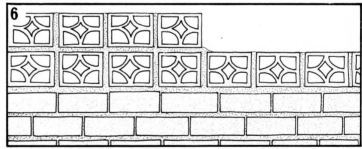

Continue cementing blocks into place from corners, checking for straightness repeatedly with spirit level. Cement second course in place as first, ensuring that mortar joins are as uniform as possible.

7

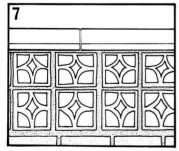

When the two courses are completed, cement coping pieces at top, matching joins but using only a thin layer of mortar.

8

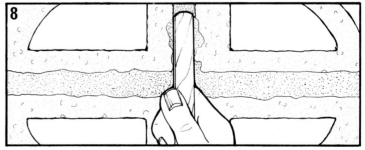

When mortar is starting to set, neaten joins by gently running a rounded stick first down, then along the joins. Brush off the surplus mortar before it sets.

Patio Paving

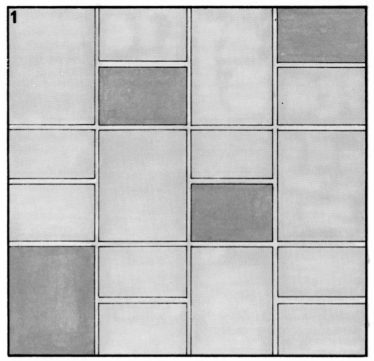

This formal pattern is not difficult to lay and makes a small, paved area appear larger. Plan your paving layout so that any broken pieces of paving are next to flowerbeds rather than walls and so that the pattern is not interrupted at patio centre.

Cover ground with a 2.5cm layer of bedding sand. Roll with garden roller for firm surface.

Lay out stones over surface in required pattern. Try not to dig holes in bedding sand when handling the stones.

At corner, place first stone flush to wall. Move next stone to within 1cm of edge of first. Tap both into place with mallet.

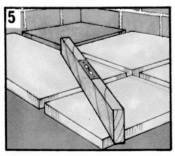

Continue laying stones until ground is covered. Use a spirit level to ensure that paving is level.

Mix mortar in stated proportion and, following manufacturer's instructions, add mortar colouring.

Fill joints between stones generously with mortar. Leave to dry. Brush off excess mortar with stiff broom.

Bamboo Lean-to

YOU WILL NEED:
1.25cm-diameter bamboo poles:
  2 × 370cm; 2 × 243cm;
  2 × 300cm; 10 × 122cm;
  and 12 × 155cm
Rawlplugs · Drill
Screwdriver · Screws
Bitumen paint
Raffia rope
Clear polyurethane varnish
Paint brush
Retractable rule
Spade

Our lean-to is centred around the garden door, but you can of course position it where you please. If you are paving your patio, remember to leave the ground uncovered at the sides of the lean-to so that you can grow climbing plants all over it.

Using rawlplugs and drill, screw two 243cm poles to house wall 370cm apart. Screw 370cm pole to wall between them.

Cover 5cm at one end of the 300cm poles with bitumen paint. Leave to dry.

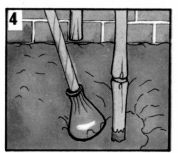

Using spade to loosen earth, insert poles 122cm away from and in line with poles on wall. Pack earth tightly round pole bases.

With raffia rope, lash 370cm crossing pole to outer uprights. (You will need help to hold pole in position.)

Lash crossing poles at corners and at 92cm intervals up sides and along the top frame.

Lash diagonal poles in place. It is fiddly to lash poles at wall edge, but slide raffia behind thin sections of bamboo.

Light Fantastic

Painted window screens are a glamorous alternative to net curtains. The light is filtered gently through and the screens can block out an unpleasing view or hide unattractive windows. They can be painted to match your woodwork, curtains or walls. Take care when painting them that blobs of paint don't collect in the decorative cut-outs.

YOU WILL NEED:
50 × 25mm wooden battens
Copper nails
Pin hammer
Panelaire*
Saw · Mitre box
2 face-fixing cabinet hinges
    with screws per window
Screwdriver
4 steel L-brackets and
    screws per window
Primer · Undercoat · Gloss paint
Swing catches

***See list of suppliers on**
    page 94

1 Measure height and width of window *within* window frame.

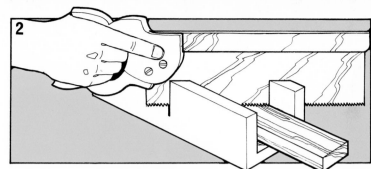

2 Cut battens to size, using mitre box to form 45° angles at each end of batten.

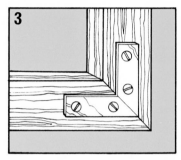

3 Screw frames together with L-brackets at corners.

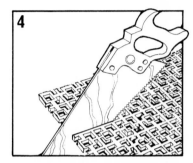

4 Cut Panelaire to size 1.25cm less in height and width than *outer* edges of frame.

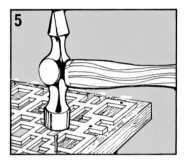

5 Nail Panelaire at 2.5cm intervals 6mm from edge, to back of frame.

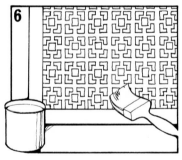

6 Prime, undercoat and paint with one coat of gloss, both sides of screen and frame. Leave to dry.

7 Screw hinges into place 15cm from top and 15cm from bottom of frame.

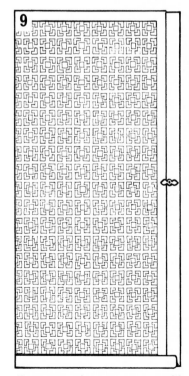

8 Making sure that *backs* of screens face window, screw hinges already positioned on screen into place on window frame.

9 If screens swing open, secure with swing catches. Screw catches in window frame at centre of outer edge of screen.

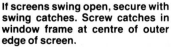

Sophisticated String

Net curtains, however pretty, can become monotonous. Here we show you an attractive alternative—woven string. Lengths of thick string woven in a variety of patterns can be purchased (see list of suppliers on page 94) and once you have followed our instructions for installing the rod, you can ring the changes with bead or bamboo curtains. Order a brass case rod from your suppliers, cut to the length of your window, measured from edge to edge of the inside of the frame.

This treatment is also suitable for doors where you want to screen off a glass door with the minimum loss of light, or create an illusion of space whilst separating rooms.

YOU WILL NEED:
For windows:
2 face-fix sockets
15mm-diameter brass case
  rod
Screwdriver · Screws
Lengths of woven string the
  height of window

For doors:
2 end-fix sockets
15mm brass case rod
Screwdriver · Screws
Plastic wood or filler
Sandpaper
Gloss paint

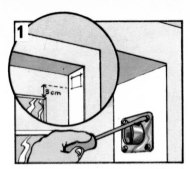

1 Mark off for fittings at each side of window frame 5cm above top of window. Screw fittings into place.

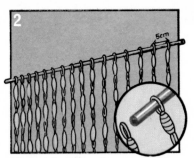

2 Thread lengths of woven string, cut to required lengths, on to rod. Allow for 5cm gaps between the lengths when in position.

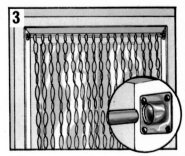

3 Affix tube with threaded lengths into fittings.

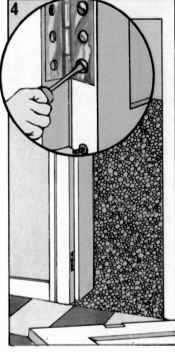

4 Unscrew door hinges. Remove door and hinges from frame.

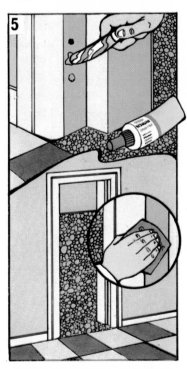

5 Make good any holes in frame by stopping up with plastic wood or filler. Sand when dry.

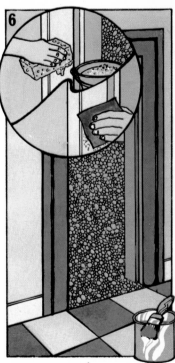

6 Wash, rub down with glasspaper and repaint door frame with one coat of gloss.

7 Mark off for fittings at inside centre of door frame 5cm from the top. Screw fittings into place.

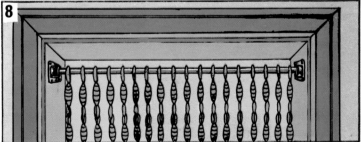

8 Thread woven string on to rod as in box 2 and install rod in fittings. For variety, you can cut the string so that it has an uneven lower edge.

Shoji Screens

These rice-paper screens come from Japan, where they are widely used for windows and garden doors. They are light, easy to install and can easily be folded away when not required. We show you how to make a three-panelled screen for a window, each panel measuring 152.4cm high × 46cm wide. Check your own window measurement, measuring from edge to edge of the frame, but do not make any panel wider than 61cm. You can make door screens in the same way.

YOU WILL NEED:
13m wooden batten,
   50 × 25mm
5.25m wooden batten,
   25 × 25mm
Saw · Mitre box
Screwdriver · Screws
Staple gun · Staples
2.50m rice paper, 1m wide
Primer · Undercoat · Black
   gloss paint
Paint brush
Retractable rule
6.50mm cabinet hinges
Glue

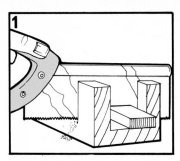

1 For panel frame, saw 50 × 25mm batten into two pieces of 46cm and two of 152.4cm. Use mitre box for 45° ends.

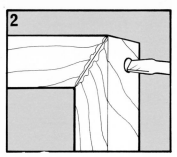

2 Screw and glue lengths together at corners to form outer frame.

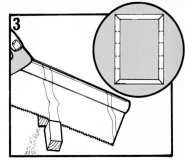

3 Saw 25 × 25mm batten into four lengths of 45cm each. Mark off outer frame at 35cm intervals.

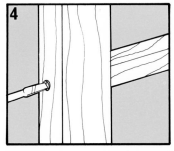

4 Screw crossing battens into place at marked intervals.

5 Prime and undercoat frame, then paint with one coat of black gloss. Leave to dry.

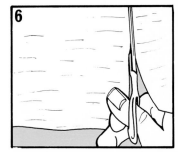

6 Cut rice paper into a length 152.4cm high × 46cm wide.

7 Using staple gun, staple rice paper to frame all round edge at 5cm intervals.

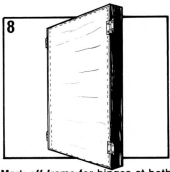

8 Mark off frame for hinges at both sides, 35cm from top and bottom. Screw hinges into marked positions.

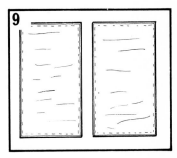

9 Make up two more panels, following instructions for the first.

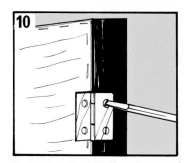

10 Mark off each side of centre panel for hinges, 35cm from top and bottom. Screw hinges to right-hand edge of panel.

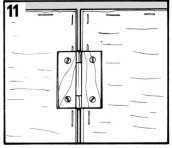

11 Mark off left-hand edge of last panel for hinges. Screw panel to centre panel.

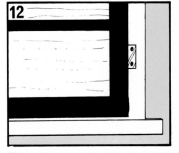

12 Offer up screen to window and mark for hinges on window frame. Screw screen into place on window frame.

Open and Closed Doors

Several of our projects have shown exciting and different things to do with windows. Now we show you some ideas for doors. Doors are a neglected feature of home décor, and flush doors especially can be a place for adventurous designs. The following ideas are suitable for cupboard as well as room doors. Decorating a door is a good project to tackle when you haven't got the time or energy for a bigger job, and you will be surprised what a difference even a small decorative touch—like our suggestion for painted finger plates—will make to your home.

YOU WILL NEED:
For the finger plates:
Clear Perspex 8cm
   wide × 23cm high*
2 domed mirror screws
Drill
Artist's oil paints
Artist's brushes
Squared paper
Pencil
Screwdriver

*See list of suppliers on
   page 94

You can either copy our designs for your finger plate or invent some of your own. Remember to colour-match with your room décor.

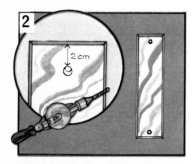

Drill two holes in Perspex at centre, 2cm from top and bottom.

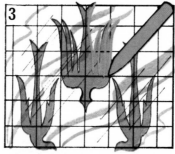

Transfer design to squared paper. 1 square in our picture equals 1cm. Trace design on to Perspex with oil paint.

Paint in solid colours. Leave to dry *thoroughly.* Screw to door above knob, painted side to the door.

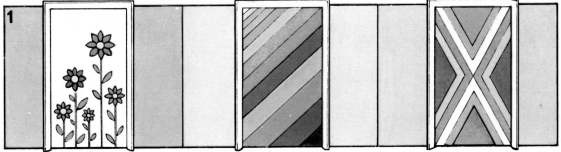

1 The designs on these doors have been painted on with a stencil. (For how to stencil, see page 17.) Ensure that your door surface is clean and smooth before you start, and do not overload your brush.

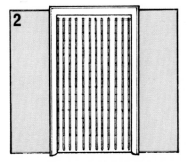
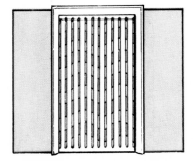
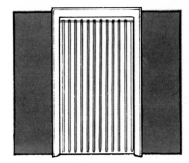

2 Here are some suggestions for beaded doors in a formal pattern. Install a rod to take the beaded lengths following our instructions on page 89. Choose heavy glass or plastic beads, which will hang better and show off a pattern.

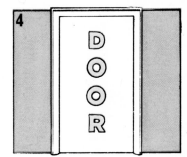

3 When you have a range of cupboards in a child's room, paint a bunny frieze on each door. For an attractive bunny design which you can scale up to different sizes see page 45.

4 Here is a fun idea for an older child. The lettering is stencilled on.

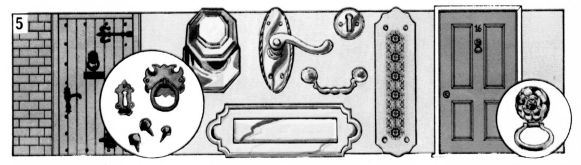

5 Brighten up your doors with purchased door furniture (see list of suppliers on page 94). Choose the style of furniture that matches the room décor, or, for a front door, the period of the house.

List of Suppliers and Manufacturers

Most of the products needed in our projects can be found in good do-it-yourself shops, but in case you have difficulty, we have listed manufacturers and importers of the more unusual products. These can be bought through your retailer if you give him the names of the firms concerned.

Wood Mouldings
These are carried by most timber merchants but you may be more successful in finding the exact moulding you want if you consult a catalogue (which your retailer will supply) from one of the larger manufacturers, like:
 General Woodwork Supplies, 76 Stoke Newington High
   Street, London N16

Decorative Carvings
The 'Softwood Carvings' featured in our project *Instant Elegance* on page 26 are available through your supplier from:
   Sefco Ltd., 6/9 Timber Street, London EC1

Panelaire
This is manufactured in the USA and is usually available from larger timber wholesalers. In case of difficulty, your supplier should contact the importing agents:
 Wright Graham Ltd., 89 Clarence Street,
   Kingston-upon-Thames, Surrey

Woven String and Bamboo Curtains
These are imported from the East by a variety of agents. Some of the most comprehensive stocks are imported through:
   Henry Gross Ltd., Maidstone Buildings, 74 Borough High
     Street, London SE1

Folding-Door Gear
The gear, with or without ready-made doors, can be ordered by your supplier from:
 Apex Enterprises, Corporation Road, Birkenhead, Cheshire
   L41 1HB
Marley supply the gear, but only *with* doors. They can be ordered by your supplier from:
   Marley, Sevenoaks, Kent

Plastic Beads
To follow our suggestions for making plastic bead door-curtains, we suggest you try your local craft shop for the beads. In case of difficulty, your shop can obtain supplies from:
    Reeves & Son Ltd., Lincoln Road, Enfield, Middlesex

Staple Guns
These are obtainable from large stationers and suppliers of office equipment. We recommend those manufactured by:
    Rexel International Ltd., 4 North Road, London N7

Perspex
This is the ICI trade name for acrylic sheet. For supplies, your retailer should contact the local wholesaler handling ICI products.

Door Furniture
Catalogues illustrating an immense range of door furniture are available from:
    J. D. Beardmore & Co. Ltd., 4 Percy Street, London W1

Hire Shops
Many towns have hire shops for building and decorating equipment and several do-it-yourself shops also offer a hire service. If you cannot trace a suitable shop in your locality, we recommend Hire Service Shops Ltd., from a whom a fully illustrated catalogue of the items available can be obtained. They have branches at:

    171/173 Station Road, Stechford, Birmingham 33;
    Unit K, Lion Industrial Estate, Atlantic Street, Broad Heath, Altrincham, Cheshire;
    45/47 Penistone Road, North Hillsborough, Sheffield;
    91/105 Leas Road, Oldham, Lancs.;
    Sloper Road, Cardiff CF1 BTG;
    865 Fulham Road, London SW6;
    42 Kingsbury Road, London NW9

Bamboo Poles
Bamboo poles in various thicknesses can be obtained from larger garden centres and horticultural suppliers.